Managing Risk in Projects

Prof Javed Iqbal Saani

PhD, MBA (MIS), MBA (Finance), BBA

Muhammad Rafi Khattak

Intellectual Capital Enterprise Limited, London

Published by Intellectual Capital Enterprise Limited, ICE Kemp House, 152-160 City Road, London, EC1V 2NX; Printed in England with the collaboration of Amazon.co.uk.

Contents

About the authors

Javed Iqbal was a resident of Rawalakot (AJ&K). He received his Ph.D. from the University of Salford and an MBA (Information Management) from the University of Hull. Previously Dr. Iqbal received BBA and an MBA (in Finance) from the University of AJ&K both with distinction. The University of Azad Jammu & Kashmir, Muzaffarabad (AJ&K) awarded him two gold medals for his educational performance. The government of Pakistan selected him for higher education and deputed him to the UK to complete

his doctorate. The government of Pakistan awarded him $100, 000 for it.

Professor Iqbal joined IQRA University Islamabad campus as an associate professor in 2006. He became the head of Department of Technology Management in International Islamic University Islamabad (IIUI) in 2012. Dr. Iqbal joined AKU (AJ&K) as a professor in 2015 and has been appointed as a Dean Faculty of Management Sciences.

His article titled "Learning from a Doctoral Research Project: Structure and Content of a Research Proposal" has been ranked by the Deakin University of Australia as the best piece of research for doctoral students. The research paper is immensely popular. Dr. Javed Iqbal has been nominated by an international organization for the Award of Distinguished Scientist for his research contribution. Professor Iqbal has published 22 research articles and 51 books so far. He has developed an interest in Islamic Leadership Style recently. Professor Iqbal has published in such International Journals as *Electronic Journal of Business Research Methods*, *European Journal of Social Sciences*, *Œconomica*, and *European Journal of Scientific Research*. His books on various subjects are available on Amazon, details are at the end of the book.

You can reach him @ iqbalsaani@gmail.com

Website: javediqbalsaani.wordpress.com

Muhammad Rafi Khattak worked as researcher with Dr Iqbal, the book is the outcome of their efforts. Contribution of Muhammad Nadeem Khan is also part of it.

Value of knowledge
Say (to them, O Muhammad(ﷺ)): Are those who know equal with those who know not? But only men of understanding will pay heed. [Az-Zumar: 9]

Value of knowledge I

Anas (May Allah (SWT) be pleased with him) reported: The Messenger of Allah (SWT) (ﷺ) said, "He who goes forth in search of knowledge is considered as struggling in the Cause of Allah (SWT) until he returns." [At- Tirmidhi]. Abu Hurairah (May Allah (SWT) be pleased with him) reported: Messenger of Allah (SWT) (ﷺ) said, "Verily! The world is accursed and what it contains is accursed, except remembrance of Allah (SWT) and those who associate themselves with Allah (SWT); and a learned person, and a learning person." [At- Tirmidhi, Book 1, Hadith 478.

Value of Knowledge II

Abu'd-Darda' (رضي الله عنه) said, "I heard the Messenger of Allah (SWT) (ﷺ), say, 1.'Allah (SWT) will make the path to the Garden easy for anyone who travels a path in search of knowledge. 2.Angels spread their wings for the seeker of knowledge out of pleasure for what he is doing. 3.Everyone in the heavens and everyone in the earth asks forgiveness for a man of knowledge, even the fish in the water. 4.The superiority of the man of knowledge to the man of worship is like the superiority of the moon to all the planets. 5.The men of knowledge are the heirs of the Prophet's (ﷺ). 6.The Prophets (AS) bequeath neither dinar nor dirham; they bequeath knowledge. Whoever takes it has taken an ample portion.'" [Abu Dawud and at-Tirmidhi; Riyadh us Salihin, Hadith 1388, p. 211]

Qualities of good leader/manager

It was by the mercy of God that you were lenient with them (O Muhammad (ﷺ)), for if you had been severe and hard-hearted, they would have forsaken you. So, pardon them and ask (God's) forgiveness for them and consult with them upon the conduct of affairs. [Al-e-Imran: 159]

Qualities of good leader/manager I

Hadhrat Ibn 'Umar (RA) reports that Rasulullah (ﷺ) said "Three persons are such as will have no fear of the horrors of the Day of Judgement, nor they will be required to render an account. They will stroll merrily on mounds of musk until the people are relieved of rendering their account. One is a person who learned the Qur'an, merely seeking Allah (SWT)'s pleasure and therewith leads people in salat in a manner that they are pleased with him; the second person is the one who invites men to salaat for the pleasure of Allah (SWT) alone. <u>The third person is the one who has fair dealings between him and his master, as well as between himself and his subordinates</u>" [Quoted by Al-Tibrani in Al-Majam Al-Slaasa; Fazail-e-Amaal, Virtues of the Holy Qur'an, Hadith 36]

Qualities of good leader/manager II

Abdullah Ibn-e-'Umar Radiy Allah (SWT) 'anhuma narrates that a person came to Nabi (ﷺ) and asked: O Rasulullah (ﷺ)! How many times may I forgive my servant? Nabi remained silent. <u>The man asked again: O Rasulullah (ﷺ)! How many times may I forgive my servant? He replied: Everyday seventy times.</u> (Tirmidhi) Note: In Arabic, the figure 'seventy' is used to express too many in number. [Muntakhib Ahadith, p. 415]

Basics of Islamic Management

And by the Mercy of Allah, you dealt with them gently. And had you been severe and harsh hearted, they would have broken away from about you; so, pass over (their faults), and ask (Allah's) Forgiveness for them; and consult them in the affairs. Then when you have taken a decision, put your trust in Allah, certainly, Allah loves those who put their trust (in Him). [Al-e-Imran: 159]

Narrated Abdullah ibn Umar: A man came to the Prophet (ﷺ) and asked: Messenger of Allah! how often shall I forgive a servant? He gave no reply, so the man repeated what he had said, but he kept silence. When he asked a third time, he replied: Forgive him seventy times daily. [Sunan Abi Dawud: Hadith 5164]

Rasulullah (ﷺ) said; 'Whenever three people proceed on a journey, one of them should be appointed as the Ameer (leader) of the group. (Mishkaat) [Fazail-e-Hajj, p. 56]

Striving for the cause of Allah (SWT)

Narrated Abu Hurairah: A man from the Companions of the Prophet (ﷺ) passed by ravine containing a small spring of thirst-quenching water, so he was amazed by how pleasant it was. So, he said: 'I should leave the people and stay in this ravine. But I will not do it until I seek permission from the Messenger of Allah (SWT) (ﷺ).' So, he mentioned that to the Messenger of Allah (SWT) (ﷺ) and he said: 'Do not do so. For indeed one of you standing in the cause of Allah (SWT) is more virtuous that his Salat in his house for seventy years. Do you not love that Allah (SWT) forgive your sins and admit you into Paradise? Then fight in the cause of Allah

(SWT), for whoever fights in Allah (SWT)'s cause for the time it takes for two milking of a camel, then Paradise is obligatory for him.'" [Jami` at-Tirmidhi: English translation: Vol. 3, Book 20, Hadith 1650]

Enjoining piety is a·sadaqah.

Sayyiduna Abu Dbarr (RA) narrated that Allah's (SWT) Messenger (ﷺ) said," With the beginning of morning, sadaqah becomes due on every. bone of each of you. So, every tasbih is a sadaqah, every tahmid is a sadaqah, every takbir is a sadaqah, enjoining piety is a sadaqah. All that may be replaced by two raka'at (Cycles) one offers for the salah of duha." [Mazahir-i-Haq (Translation & Commentary of MISHKA TUL MASAABIH), Hadith 1311, V. 1, p. 778.]

Greatness of Allah (SWT)

Allah (SWT), the Exalted *in the name of Allah (SWT), the Beneficent, the Merciful*.1. All that is in the heavens and the earth glorifieth Allah (SWT); and He is the Mighty, the Wise. 2. His is the Sovereignty of the heavens and the earth; He quickeneth and He giveth death, and He can do all things. 3. He is the First and the Last, and the Outward and the Inward, and He is Knower of all things. 4. He is Who created the heavens and the earth in six Days; then He mounted the Throne. He knoweth all that entereth the earth and all that emergeth therefrom and all that cometh down from the sky and all that ascendeth therein, and He is with you wheresoever ye may be. And Allah (SWT) is Seer of what ye do. 5. His is the Sovereignty of the heavens and the earth, and unto Allah (SWT) (all) things are brought back. 6. He causeth the night to pass into the day, and He causeth the day to pass into the night, and He is the knower of all that is in the breasts. [Al-Hadidh: 1-6]

Allah (SWT) likes those who love one another. Yahya related to me from Malik from Abu Hazim ibn Dinar that Abu Idris al-Khawlani said, "I entered the Damascus Mosque and there was a young man with a beautiful mouth and white teeth sitting with some people. When they disagreed about something, they referred it to him and proceeded from his statement. I inquired about him, and it was said, 'This is Muadh ibn Jabal.' The next day I went to the noon-prayer, and I found that he had preceded me to the noon prayer, and I found him praying. "Abu Idris Al-Khaulani (May Allah (SWT) had mercy upon him) reported: I once entered the mosque in Damascus. I happened to catch sight of a young man who had bright teeth (i.e., ., he was always seen smiling). Several people had gathered around him. When they differed over anything, they would refer it to him and act upon his advice. I asked who he was, and I was told that he was Mu'adh bin Jabal (May Allah

(SWT) be pleased with him) The next day I hastened to the mosque but found that he had arrived before me and was busy in performing Salat. I waited until he finished, and then went to him from the front, greeted him with Salam and said to him, "By Allah (SWT) I love you." He asked, "For the sake of Allah (SWT)?" I replied, "Yes, for the sake of Allah (SWT)". He again asked me, "Is it for Allah's (SWT) sake?" I replied, "Yes, it is for Allah (SWT)'s sake." Then he took hold of my cloak, drew me to himself and said, "Rejoice! I heard Messenger of Allah (SWT) (ﷺ) saying, *'Allah (SWT), the Exalted, says: My love is due to those who love one another for My sake, meet one another for My sake, visit one another for My sake and spend in charity for My sake"*. [Riyad as-Salihin: English book reference: Book 1, Hadith 382] (Muwatta Malik: English reference: Book 51, Hadith 15)

Dedication

To our parents who invested heavily for our education and remained engaged in prayers for my success and wellbeing.

Acknowledgment

Special gratitude is due to all those who helped me to compile the work. I am grateful to my family who spared me to embark on the project. They also supply valuable information which enriched the contents of this effort.

I am obliged to pay my gratitude to honourable faculty members of International Islamic University Islamabad Prof Dr Muhammad Bashir Khan (ex-Vice president and dean of the Faculty of Management Sciences), Dr Abdul Zahid Khan, acting chairman of the Department of Technology Management (Faculty of Management Sciences) Dr Zubair Sarfraz, Advocate Islamabad High Court, and Prof Habib Tabeti of the University Mustapha Stambouli of Mascara, Algeria for their encouragement and support for the work. May Allah (SWT) reward them for their contribution? Ameen! Contribution of Muhammad Nadeem Khan in the earlier edition of the book is also acknowledgeable which contains this edition as well.

Preface

Project managers are constraints on cost, quality, and in-time quality; quality of projects is associated with corresponding increase in cost. Similarly, in-time completion of a project pressurizes both cost and quality.

In addition, managers meet risk the fourth constraints. Risk is the probability in the variation of resources, unforeseen events and changes in government regulations or requirements. Project managers must foresee, figure out and manage it to achieve triple constraints and objectives of their endeavors.

We have (two of the authors) examined the basics of project management in *understanding project management*, published by Grass Books. One of our colleagues worked on risk in projects. This book is the outcome of that effort; the earlier work is the context for risk in projects. Case study 2 supports the topic. Some improvements have been made to chapter one; two new case studies have been added (the case study 2 & 3) in the original contents.

There is a plethora of literature on the subject, which focuses it from various perspectives. This book has been designed for busy people since it is a brief work, and it presents three real life case studies conducted by the authors to test the concepts empirically. The case studies have been taken from the service industry and small businesses which makes the book unique from the available literature.

We welcome comments and suggestions from academia and practitioners for further improvements in the future.

Dr. Javed Iqbal Saani

Muhammad Rafi Khattak

12 April 2011, Islamabad

Preface to the second edition

The purpose of the book is to look at project management from a risk management perspective. We have investigated the fundamentals of project management and added a case study about project management from an Islamic perspective in this volume. For this purpose, we have selected the hijrah of the prophet (ﷺ) as a case study to understand the Islamic viewpoint of the subject. The principal author has investigated the topic in a separate book;[1] however, it looks proper to include the case study in this revised edition of one-of my earlier books which I have compiled with the help of my colleagues. I hope that this will be beneficial for our readers and enhance the understanding of professionals in this field.

The reference pattern of the new case was in footnotes manner; therefore, it stays as it is for the convenience of the readers. The font size is 11 and 12 because of editing requirements/limitations.

Prof Dr. Javed Iqbal Saani

30 July 2022, Manchester

---

[1] Javed Iqbal Saani (2021) *Project Management: An Islamic Perspective,* Intellectual Capital Enterprise Limited, London, available on Amazon (Paperback edition)

1 INTRODUCTION

Learning objectives

- Understand the nature of project

- Explain the role of projects manager

- Describe the arena of project management as a modern discipline

- Know the importance of managing projects systematically

- Understand the evolution of project management as a separate discipline

Nature of projects

Juran (1989) views a project as a schedule for solution. A schedule dines the activities and corresponding time of doing that activity, starting, or finishing. This view assumes timing dimension. However, a project is more than that and normally includes many other elements. Andersen (1995) and his colleagues believe a project is a combination of a unique task, is chosen to achieve a specific result, requires a variety of resources, and limited in time. Project management institute defines it

Box 1: Project

View I

Project is a problem discovered by senior managers, customer, partners, imposed by competitors, emerged because of government policies, natural disasters etc. It needs a solution and a project is a schedule for that solution.

View II

Project is a unique task, may emerge once in life time of a person
Designated to achieve specific objectives
Requires resources
Bound in time limit

View III

Project is a temporary endeavor
It has beginning and ending dates
Creates a product or service

Learning (synthesis)

A project is a unique temporary problem to be resolved by an individual or organization within a given time with appropriate resources.

as temporary endeavor with definitive beginning and ending and creation of a unique product or service (PMI, 2004). A project's uniqueness separates it from routine work and other projects being undertaken in an organization. For example, development of a website for a university is a specific and on-off job of a website developer. A project is also meant to achieve one or more objectives: efficiency, profitability or customer satisfaction. All that need resources: human, financial, plant & machinery, methods, techniques, information, and a plan. Finally, it is bounded by time: a day, a week, a month or a year.

Project management

Project management is "the application of knowledge, skills, tools, and techniques to project requirements" (PMI, 2004). Project management is "The planning, organization, monitoring and control of all aspects of a project and the motivation of all involved to achieve the project objectives safely and within agreed time, cost and performance criteria. The project manager is the single point of responsibility for achieving this." (UK BoK, 1995)

Box 2: Project Management

View I

The application of knowledge, skills, tools, and techniques to project requirements.

View II

The planning, organization, monitoring and control of all aspects of a project and the motivation of all involved to achieve the project objectives safely and within agreed time, cost and performance criteria.

View III

Project management involves, planning, organizing and controlling of a project.

Learning (synthesis)

Projects management is the application of managerial functions and capabilities as well as available technologies for the completion of a specific project within agreed upon constraints (cost, budget, time).

Andersen and his colleagues (1995) argue that project management involves planning, organizing, and controlling. Planning involves deciding in advance what to do, when to do, where to do, who is to do. Planning is the first step; hence, its effectiveness influences later phases and the performance of the project as well as organization. Organizing encompasses assigning the responsibilities of a project team to constituent members after building such a team. And controlling involves ensuring that things are done according to plan; and taking corrective actions in case of any discrepancy.

Project management is a broad term applicable to the national and international levels; when two or more nations undertake an organized venture with clear objectives, resources and time frame, it may be called an international project. United Nations starts projects in developing countries to reduce poverty or enhance welfare of people. Sometimes business organizations undertake a project with international companies; British Aerospace (BAe), developed EU2000 fighter with the help of German, Italian and Spanish partners. There are also some examples of project undertaken by a political or economic block of countries such as OPEC, EU, ASEAN, SAARC etc.; they are multinational projects.

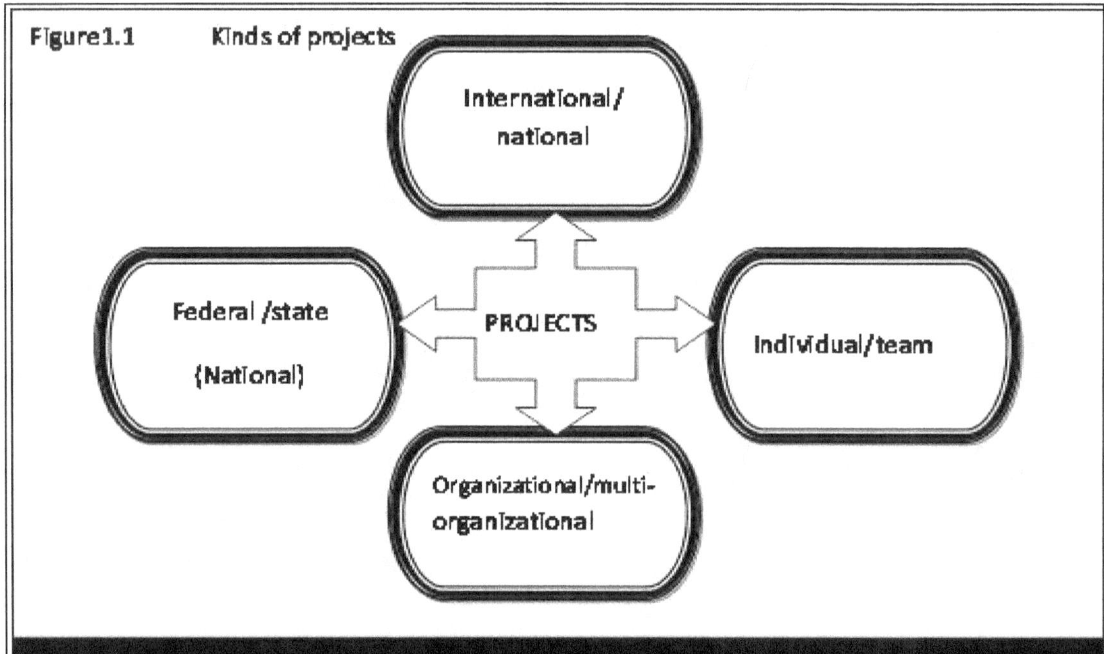

Apart from that, countries start national or provisional projects according to their political system of government. Any project undertaken by the federal government is a federal project and any project undertaken by any of the states is a state project (See Figure 1 .1 above).

Country based projects are started to improve communication, construction, education, defense capability, social welfare, health, and social responsibility. Their purpose is to increase the facilities of the nation and enhance the standard of living of people or quality of life. Business organizations launch projects to increase the wealth of owners (See Figure 1.2). They work as a machine to generate added resources to inject fresh blood into the body of the organizational machine to keep it healthy and make the company wealthy. Business organizations launch a project with the assumption that it will be workable, profitable, and manageable. The purpose of feasibility study prior to launching a project is to confirm or make sure that the assumptions are achievable within the resource constraints and time involved. Business organizations normally initiate projects for a range of goals (See Figure 1.3).

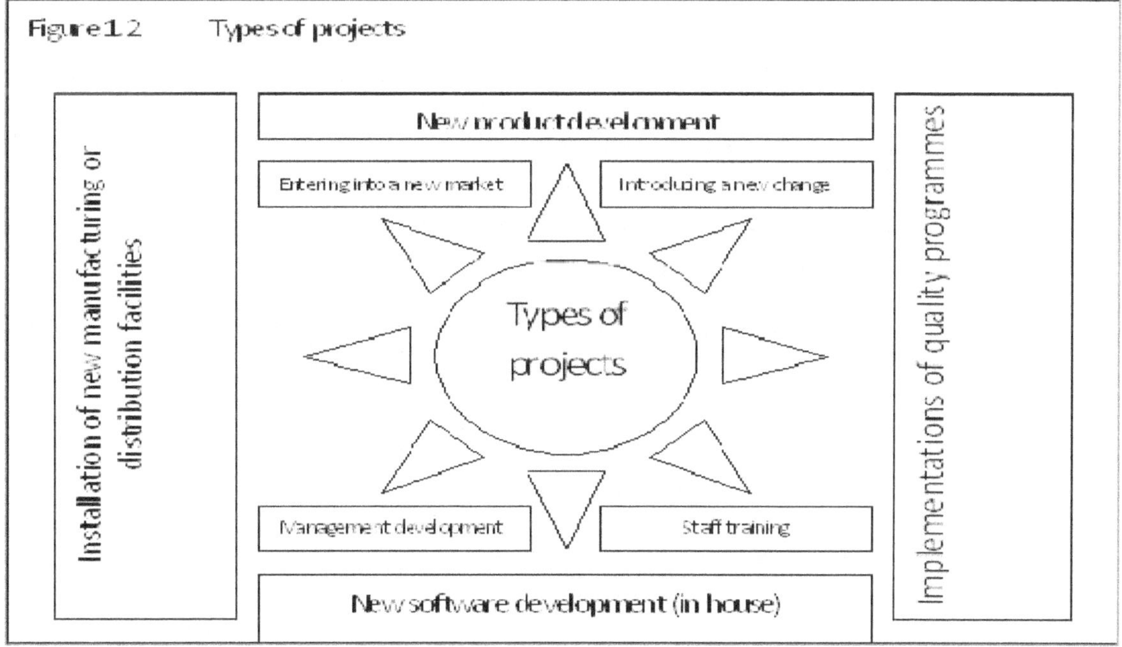

Each of the above projects requires unique combination of resources according to their requirements (See Figure 1.4).

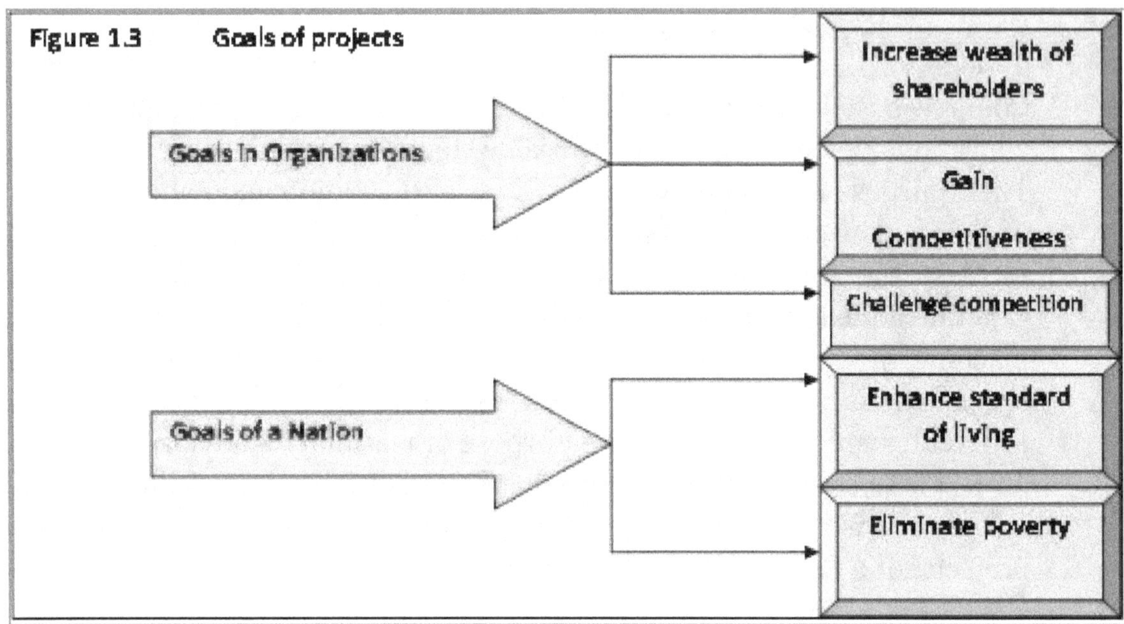

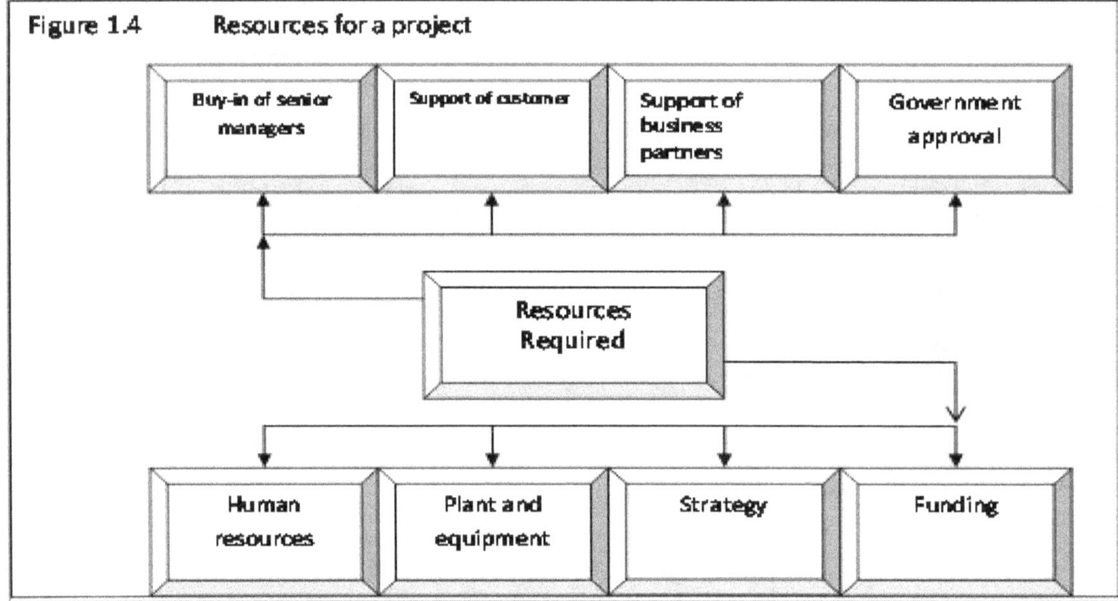

For example, quality means consistency of outcomes according to the standard defined. Companies manufacture and deliver products through one or more business processes; each process must implement quality standards to achieve efficiency and competitiveness in the industry. A company must introduce new projects to support its business network, suppliers, and customers. The success and failure of a vital project creates impacts on the businesses of these organizations.

It may be worthwhile to remember that country level projects aiming at national development are different from organizational projects in that the resources are limited at organizational level than the national level. The outcome of a project in an organization is much more risky than national projects; the nations can cope with failure of a project, but an organization may not. There are many examples of projects whose failure led an organization to the jaws of bankruptcy or long-term turmoil. While many nations of the world lost resources on a venture that ended up in humiliation, failure, and loss of enormous amount of human and monetary resources. The United States lost thousands of personnel and billions of dollars in foreign wars; nevertheless, such failure did not threaten the existence of the country or did not put existence at risk. It gives project managers a serious message that they should plan and implement a project very carefully to avoid such circumstances.

Need of project management

Project management offers tangible and intangible value to organizations; the former may be realized as return on investment, metrics of balance scorecard, and organizational competencies. Intangible gains are lies in change in corporate culture, efficiency, customer satisfaction, learning and growth, competitive advantage (Zhai et al, 2009). Thomas and Mullaly, (2007) suggest five levels of value: satisfaction, aligned use of practices, process outcomes, business outcomes and return on investment. It includes both process results and business outcome i.e., tangible financial returns to intangible organizational benefits. Andersen and Vaagaasar (2009) grouped the contribution of PM into economic, institutional and innovation perspectives. Economic benefits are figured out through cost/benefit analysis. Organizations make investment decision in their best interest which is influence by the size and the importance of projects. The societal expectations and pressure guide the flow of funds in a certain direction, the institutional perspective. The innovation perspective dictates injection of current ideas and technologies as a process of adoption of innovation. Zhai et al (2009) mapped value of project management into four categories: enterprise (improve project performance, competencies of the organization, increased revenue, cultivate personnel, improve customer relationship management, and cultivate favorable culture), customer (realize the value of the project, save project investment, and better collaborative experience), community (avoid conflicts with the community, promote economic and social development, foster talent, improve technical standards, and protect environment), and subcontractors / suppliers (Improve management and technical capabilities and develop long-term strategic but cooperative partnership). Cooke-Davies et al (2009) believes project are supposed to provide fit between organizational strategy "and the type of project that it executes in implementing its strategy." (p. 110)

Crawford and Helm (2009) identified the value of projects in government endeavors which address accountability and transparency, control and compliance, risk management, consistency in delivery, ensuring value for money and engagement of stakeholders in order to improve good governance.

Role of Project manager

Projects managers are responsible to start, design, complete and end projects. They mobilize resources, decide timings of various activities, and provide guidance to people working in the project.

Project manager is responsible to perform basic business functions such as planning, organizing, leading/directing, and controlling in project perspective. *Planning* involves deciding in advance what to do, how to do, who is to do and when to do. It is associated with a task and related time involved. Certain people are assigned specific activities or tasks. They are equipped with the necessary resources for carrying out the job. *Organizing* involves dividing the project into manageable chunks, which are performed by individuals and teams. The job of a project manager is to break the entire project into milestones, tasks or activities and then form one or more teams to manage them. Teams are formed according to the nature of the project for products, geographical regions, components of a project and by the functions or business processes. Each team must be motivated, trained, and coached for their area of responsibility. The project manager coordinates his activities with the team progress; supply guidance, resources and psychological support to keep the members of the team motivated and on the track. A project manager also provide *leadership* role to the project team(s); a leader clarifies role to his team members, define or help them to defines goals within their roles, boost up their confidence so that they can achieve their goal, and ensures that they receive rewards after achieving goals (Smith, 2007). To do that a leader must be energetic, tenacious, assertive, proactive, honest, trustworthy, well organized, intelligent, verbally fluent, self-confident, own interpersonal skills, and commercially astute (ibid, p.118). These qualities differentiate a leader from a manager. A leader must be employee oriented, takes work from people as a human being and takes care of their individual, family, and cultural beliefs. But a task-oriented manager wants to improve productivity and achieve organizational goals in a mechanistic way since he/she perceives subordinates as machines or part of a bigger machine (the company).

Controlling involves measuring performance in line with the success criteria defined in the plan of a project and taking required measures to keep the project as planned. Sometimes corrective measures are not needed because the project moves amicably; however, project manager must look at the progress of milestones or other progressive parameters to ensure the project is progressing. Alternatively, a deviation from the planned vision must be followed by corrective actions. It may include changes in time scale, milestone timing or inclusion / exclusion of activities or task, these actions are necessary to ensure project is progressing in the right direction over its life cycle in socially and economically acceptable manner. Project manager relays on progress reports provided by management information systems or in case of a large project like opening a new location or branch, project information system designed for the specific project (See Figure 1.5).

Many writers took a distinct perspective of project manager; they argue project managers must have a range of competencies in addition to the traditional function. The concept of competencies appeared from organizational competencies. Competences are positively related to project management effectiveness and project success (Hartman and Skulmoski, 1999).

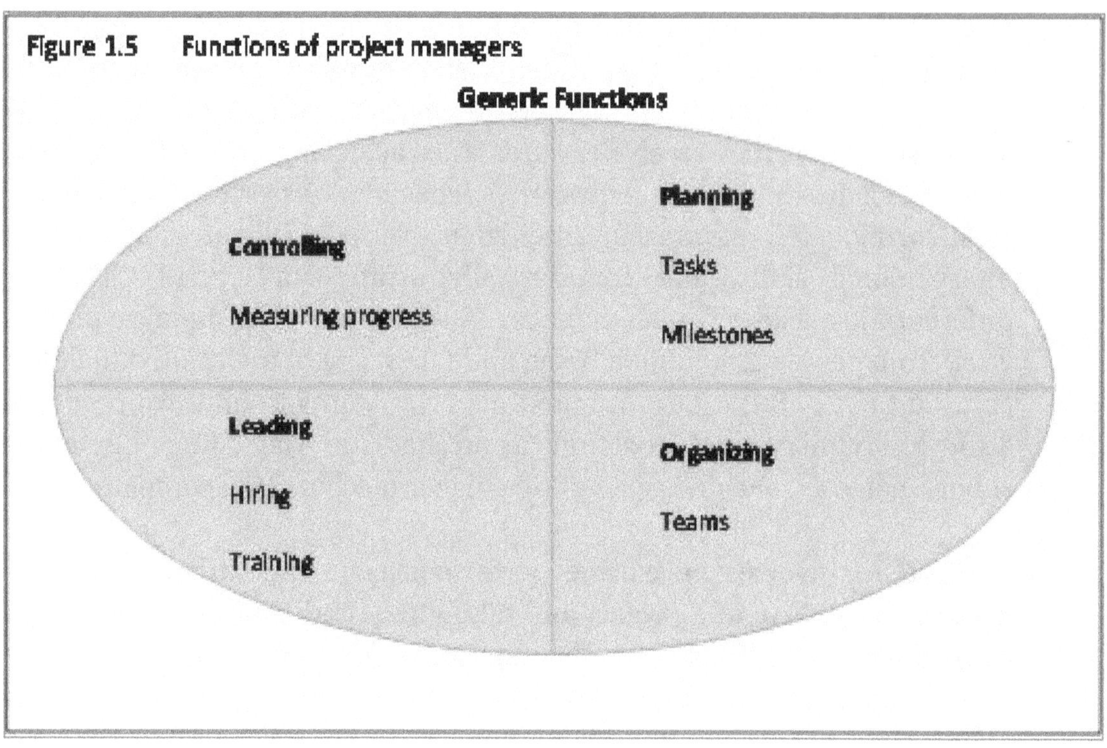

Figure 1.5   Functions of project managers

They say that project management competencies can be viewed from input-process-out framework; some competencies are needed at input level of a project (See Figure 1.6). High quality input would produce, other things being equal, high-quality output. They have taken this idea from educational institutes; for example, Oxford and Cambridge universities recruit high caliber students and polish them to produce world class output i.e., leaders, scholars, writers etc. Other organizations also follow the same strategy, NASA injects outstanding graduates into its space and related programmes.

According to Hartman and his colleague (1999) input competencies include knowledge, skills, traits, motives, self-image, social role, and behavior. Knowledge refers to the specific ability about project management, mostly imparted by chartered institutes such as project management institute (PMI). The computer age brought software tools in addition to the PMI certification; Microsoft's Project software is easily accessible and handy to learn as a primary instrument. There is a plethora of software in the current market

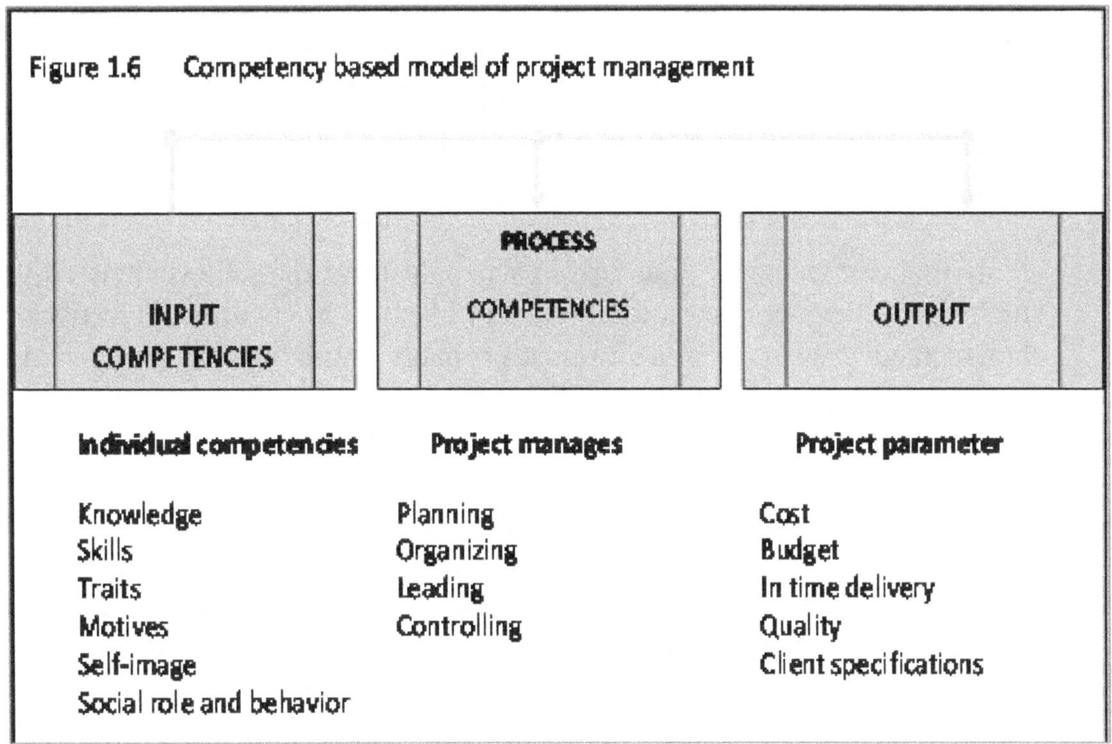

Thus, generic knowledge or certification is the first step towards project management. A related competency is the necessary skill(s) related with the profession; Hartman and Skulmoski (1999) believe it is the ability to figure out critical path in the project network. It may encompass other subjective abilities in PM perspective such as estimating time-period of an activity based on earlier experience or involvement in similar assignments. Many elements of cost determination also need insight on the part of a project manager; the amount or quantity of other non-human resources also needs subjective estimates. In addition, variations (variances) and deviation under uncertain conditions need non-quantitative approach. Project managers also function as leader who is to keep team members motivated; the level of motivation may be measured by some quantitative parameters such as absences, unit of output etc. However subjective matters like taking interest in project plans, activities and meetings can be judge by a prudent manager since there are little mechanistic instruments available and applicable in small projects or in small organization due to affordability or other reasons.

Traits are another input variable in the process. A trait according to Boyatzis (1982) as referred by Hartman and Skulmoski (1999) is a "characteristic way in which a person responds to a set of stimuli." For example, when she/he discovers a problem, tries to find its solution. This type of person is a problem solver, problem solving trait makes him distinct from others.

Motives drive behavior that inspires people towards achievements; motivated manager achieve project and individual objective. Measurable objectives need to be assigned to such a manager, most probably in the beginning of a venture and can also be reinforced during the life cycle of a project. However, it is mandatory for senior managers (or project manager for his/her team members) to keep the project teams motivated.

The final input competency is the self-image; it is the feeling of a person about himself or herself. How well is a certain person contributing towards the success or completion of a particular task? Sometimes it is perceived as a social role in a society, group or organization; the more it conforms to the societal norms the more it is appreciated and vice versa. Self-image in this contest creates self-control, a rare commodity in the market of management (See Figure 1.7).

Process competencies have extensively examined in project management literature that is normally concerned with planning, controlling, and closing of project. This book takes them elsewhere in detail.

The final aspect of the model is the output of a project; the well-known outcomes are cost, quality, contents and in time delivery. Completion of a project within an acceptable range of these dimensions lead to customers / client satisfaction since the outcome is associated with project success criteria or project objectives outlined in the outset. There are three levels of performance: individual, team (there may be more than one team working in a project, for example, in change initiatives sometimes three teams are involved: design, implementation and

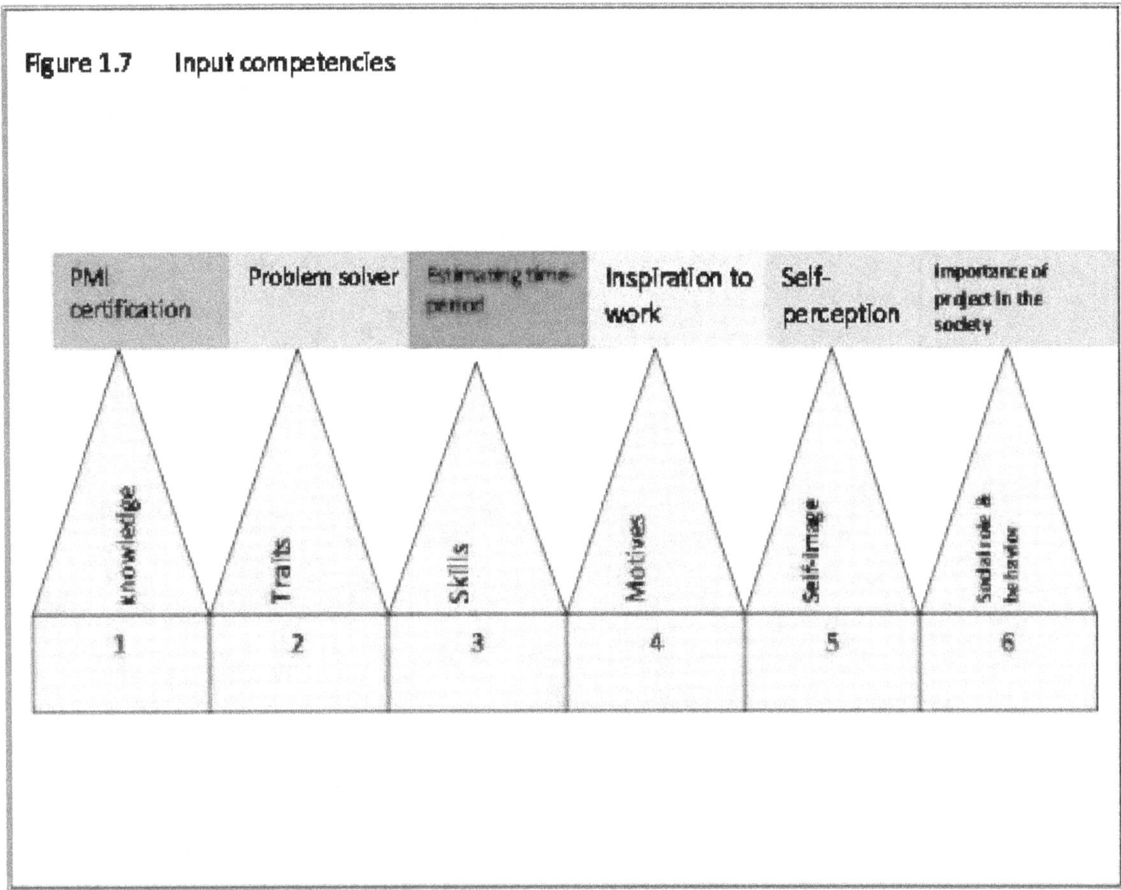

continuous improvement), and overall project performance. A project is an organized set of activities; sometimes performed sequentially but not necessarily. It is a system, that is, "a set of interrelated parts that function to achieve a common purpose" where each part "would have an impact on other parts and the entire system that can work effectively if the individual parts work effectively and cooperative." (Smith, 2007). However, the project manager compromise about high performance of some components against low performance of other components provided the sum is equal to the success criteria (Box Three).

Job description of project manager

The job descriptions of a project manager have been described under a range of capabilities. They have been broadly grouped into four categories: project/practice related competencies (project management, project accounting), career path core competencies (financial management, business development, communication, technical understanding), professional qualities (leadership,)

Box 3 The Project manager

View I

A project managers is the one who
Initiate projects
Design alternative solutions
Complete a specific unique endeavor
Terminate projects within project triangle
Mobilize organizational resources from various sources
Decide timings of activities i.e. beginning and ending as per schedule
Provide guidance to people working in the project and keep them motivated

View II
Every manager is responsible for basic business functions in addition to the specific job. Planning, organizing, leading / directing and controlling are basic and fundamental function of a manager.

View III
Project managers must possess a range of competencies in addition to the traditional function.

Learning (Synthesis)
Project manager is an individual or team who posses project related competencies and capabilities for initiation, planning, execution and control of an endeavor as defined by the organization or customer.

teamwork, and client management), organizational responsibilities (innovator development, and internal operations) (www.marisaleseanerou.com, 2010) A specific list of description has been provided by totaljobs.com (See Table 1.1). And Table 1.2 supplies a list of skills and interests needed for a project manager.

Table 1.1	Specific duties of a project manager
Key Themes	Details
Requirement capturing	The client or company's achievement out of a specific project
Resourcing	Deciding the time, cost, and resources
Planning	Writing a detailed plan to achieve various stages (milestones of the project concerned)
Team management	Finding right people for the right job and providing them leadership
Negotiating	Making arrangement for acquisition of material and services.
Progress tracking	Ensuring the progress of the project within agreed cost, time, and quality standards
Communicating and reporting	Conveying project progress to senior management or clients regularly

...

Table 1.2	Skills and intcrests of project manager
Category	Details
Managerial	Organization, planning and time management.
Problem solving	Ability to critical thinking and solving problems creatively
IT Skills	Able to manage project management software in addition to basic IT skills,

	MS office, the internet e-mail etc.
Focused approach	Able to pay attention to details
Budget control	Understanding and able to control generic and project budget
Technical skills	Relevant to the project, a PMI qualification is advisable
Business sense	Able to understand cons and pros of business world

Besides this basic knowledge and understanding, project managers should obtain either qualification or membership of professional bodies and organizations. Recommended organization includes Association for Project Management (APM), Project Management Institute (PMI), Chartered Management Institute (CMI), and Information System Examination Board (ISEB) for project management in the IT industry. Finally, is the practical experience and insight into the job.

Project management in perspective

Alshawi and Ingirige (2003) describe the historical development of project management including many different magnitudes that have been undertaken successfully across generations. Project management first emerged in the early 1950s on large defense projects and gradually smaller organizations started to adapt the idea, and currently, the smallest construction firms are known to operate project management in some form. A great deal of project management involves avoiding problems, tackling new ground, managing a group of people, and trying to achieve truly clear objectives quickly and efficiently.

The first era is known as craft system and human relations that is characterized with technological developments to shorten the length of schedule. Job specifications were developed with became the basis of work breakdown structure later in the project management era.

The second era is called the application of concepts of management science in the field of project management. Note able developments include introduction of critical path method (CPM) and programme education and review technique (PERT). The purpose of CPM was to find the most efficient way to complete a project. The technique was developed by DuPont Corporation in 1957 to resolve the problem of chemical plant maintenance.

Advantages of CPM include:

- It provides a graphical view of various activities to grasps a quick view of a project from start to end mostly on a single page.

- It can predict the completion time of a project by satisfying all the requirements at activity level. Each activity is assigned the time it needs to complete and its contribution to the entire project. It helps project managers and their team members to conceptualize the project journey with estimated time slots over the life cycle of their project prior to the start of an endeavor.

- It also highlights the critical activities and non-critical activities. Critical activities use the actual time associated with them while noncritical activities can be completed during (parallel to the critical activities) the critical activities. In this way, time is saved that is spent on non-critical activities. The emphasis is on critical activities so that the schedule may be kept. It does not mean noncritical activities are important or do not need completion; the difference arises in term of total time needed to complete a project while the period of non-critical activities become part of the critical activities.

The CPM looks like a network of activities and events; the activities are shown as nodes and events are depicted as activities on lines. PERT was also introduced during the period, which is another planning tool for project management.

The third period started in 1980 and ended in around the first half of the last decade of the dying century. Invention and affordability of personal computer and associated technologies was notable development in the period. Low cast multi-tasking and nctworking helped project managers to address complex project scheduling issues. Networking technologies enable various stakeholders to share project information over the desktop, shortening the communication gap and boosting possibilities of delivering the project on time. Project management software was available at affordable prices especially to small businesses.

The last period of development commenced with the commercialization of the internet in the mid-nineties; a period of fast interactive and customized new environment, it enables project managers and other related parties to brows, purchase and track products as well as projects 24/7 with virtually no cost.

Project management software can be connected with the Internet; it allows automatic uploading of project data so that people can input assigned task, find out the progress of the project, able to know any delays or advances in the schedule, and work for a project in addition to their routine assignments even from their own homes (See Figure 1.8).

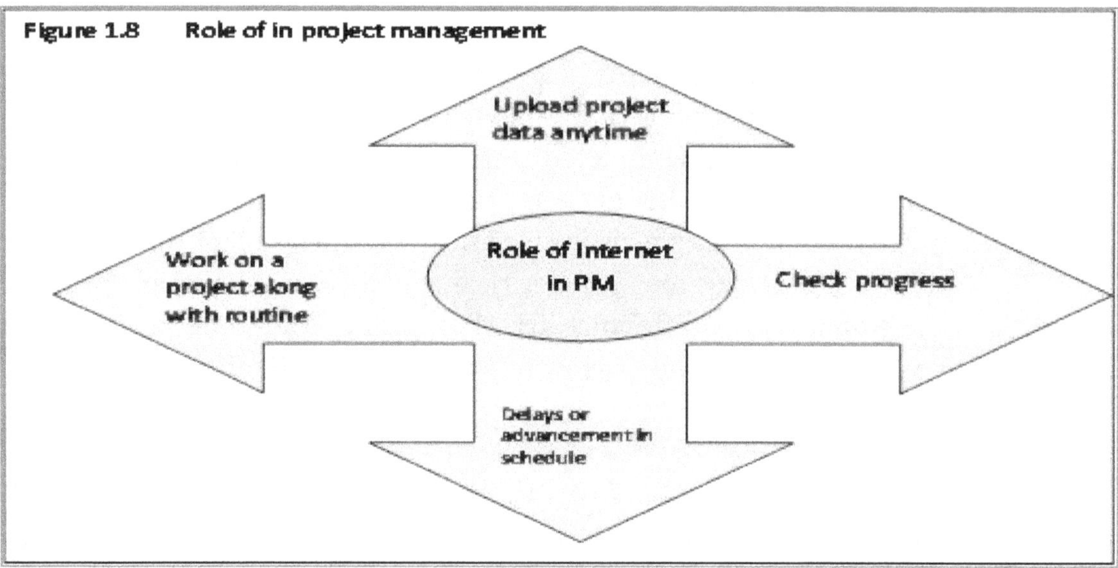

In short, this era is characterized with productivity, efficiency and client orientation thus focused on project triangle: cost, quality and in time delivery. It opens more dimensions for research and development in project planning, organization, and control. Haughey (2010) has compiled other developments in project management (See Figure 1.9).

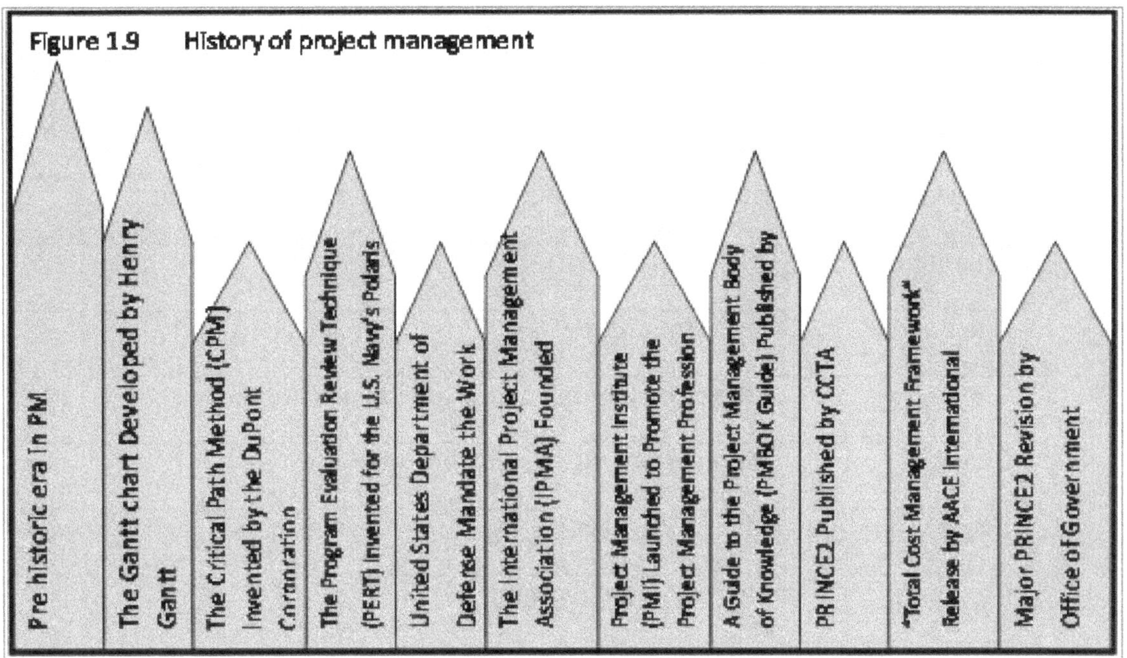

Structure of the book

The book has been organized into seven chapters. The first chapter deals with fundamentals of project management, historical developments over time, functions of projects managers and the nature of a project. Chapters 2-5 deal with the core elements of project management; they are based on the idea of UK Association of Project Management who believed that key functions of project management are project planning, organizing and control. The planning has been divided into two chapters 2 and 3. The first of them examines initiation where emphasis is one project selection, alignment with business strategy and project initiation documents. Chapter 3 describes essentials of project planning; elements of a project plan are the significant topics in the chapter. Chapter four has basics of project organizing; distributions of tasks / activities and managing or organizing other resources are the important topics. Chapter 5 is reserved for project monitoring and controlling; the key topics include basics of control, control techniques and success and failure factors. The next chapter is for the case study that incorporates all the aspects of the subject. The last chapter explains the conclusion and learning gained from the experience. Table 1.1 summarizes the description of these elements.

Table 1.1	The structure of the book
Chapter number	**Name**
Chapter 1	Introduction to the world of Project Management
Chapter 2	Project initiation
Chapter 3	Project planning
Chapter 4	Project organizing and resource allocation
Chapter 5	Project monitoring and control
Chapter 6	Risk in Projects
Chapter 7	Summary and learning
	Case studies

Review questions

1. A project is undertaken in an organization by its people; find relationship between the two.

2. Project manager is more a general manager than a project champion. Discuss.

3. Project management is a discipline older than the known history. Do you agree? Why? And why not?

4. Projects contribute to the finance of an organization only. Explain.

5. Projects management increases the complexities in organization. Evaluate.

2 PROJECT INITIATION

Learning objectives

- Know the common stakeholders of a project in the contemporary environment

- Learn the key project selection criteria both qualitative and quantitative.

- Understand the way the subjective techniques may be used as an objective approach.

- Explain the strategy of aligning new projects with existing business strategy.

- Learn how to develop a project portfolio

- Describe project identification document and its contents

Introduction

Since a project is a temporary endeavor within a given time, therefore, it can be assumed that more than one project may be in progress. Each project has a beginning and ending dates and at least an objective to satisfy its stakeholders (See Table 2.1) and produce a one-off outcome: software, a building, a road and repair to a car. They must be distinguishable from one another to manage them effectively; the distinction is made in project planning, organizing, and controlling.

Every project has a different plan, organized in one or more teams, and needs separate measures for controlling. This chapter examines initiation where emphasis is on project selection, project initiation document, and alignment with business strategy.

Table 2.1 Selected Stakeholder of a project	
Internal	**External**
Managers	Partners
Employees	Public
Entrepreneur	Customer
Internal customer	Government

Project initiation

Project initiation is a process of evaluation and choice of projects, which contributes to the overall strategy of the organization. According to the Meredith and Mantel (2010) "project initiation begins with the judicious selection of the organization's project to align them with the organization's overall strategy." Two components are important in the above statement: project selection and aligning with business strategy. Project selection begins with identification of one or more projects, senior management may suggest some project i.e.,. replacing infrastructure of information technology in an educational institution for modernization and improvement of efficiency.

Project selection

Selecting a project precedes with evaluation: the selection is made on the bases of contribution of a project towards financial or non-financial objectives of the organization. Project selection criteria may be numeric or non-numeric, sometime known as subjective and objective or qualitative and quantitative.

Qualitative approaches

When the rationality is set aside and non-economic reasons because the bases of project evaluation; the subjective guidelines supply the criteria. Meredith and his colleague (2010) put forward an array of subjective methods: senior managers suggest a project which is also known as the sacred cow, project is necessary to continue business (the operating necessity i.e., flood is threatening the company premises, therefore, a defensive wall is essential), remain competitive, (business process redesign was adopted by scores of organization because the rivals were doing it), expansion of the product line (it is usually a part of expansion policy or keeping customer fresh i.e., . the company is abreast to competition), and employee welfare benefit projects (establishment of daycare centre, a cafeteria, a hospital, a school etc.) (See Figure 2.1). Management cannot quantify their benefits but such projects are perceived beneficial for one or more of the above reasons.

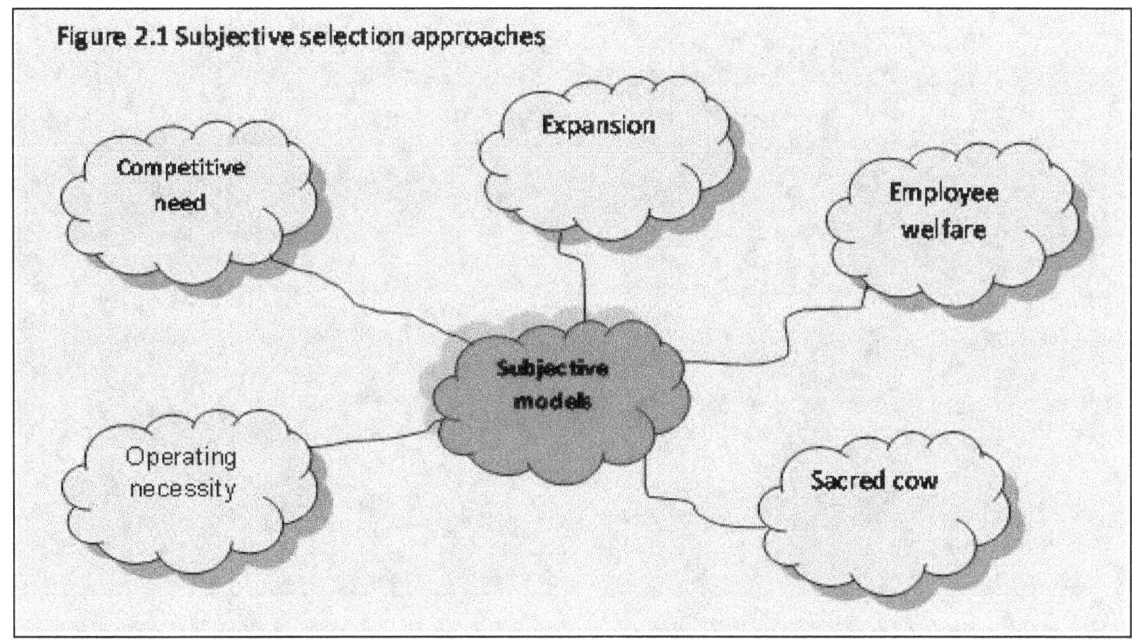

Quantitative models

These techniques are on the other end of the continuum; projects are selected on the bases of facts. Some of them are known as accounting method such as payback period (how long the project would take to recover investment; the project with short period are considered favorable), discounted cash flow (what is the net present value of discounted cash flow, the project with positive net present value are acceptable), internal rate of return (IRR) (an alternative discounted cash flow approach; the higher the IRR the more favorable it is and vice versa), profitability index (ratio of cost and benefits; a ratio greater than one is considered acceptable). (See Figure 2.2)

A variation of quantitative models is based upon numerical scores. The scoring models take into account multiple criteria for selection; they assign numerical values to different components or contributing factor; the project with higher score are selected. Sometimes a checklist is prepared including elements to be considered for choice (most of these factors may be subjective). For instance, to capture potential market share, effect on company image, no increase in energy requirements etc. (Meredith and Mental, 2010). These techniques are both un-weighted factors scoring model and weighted scoring model etc. Table 2.2 shows a hypothetical case where some selected factors were assigned scores to choose the project. In practice, the factors depend upon the circumstances of the organization or choice of senior managers.

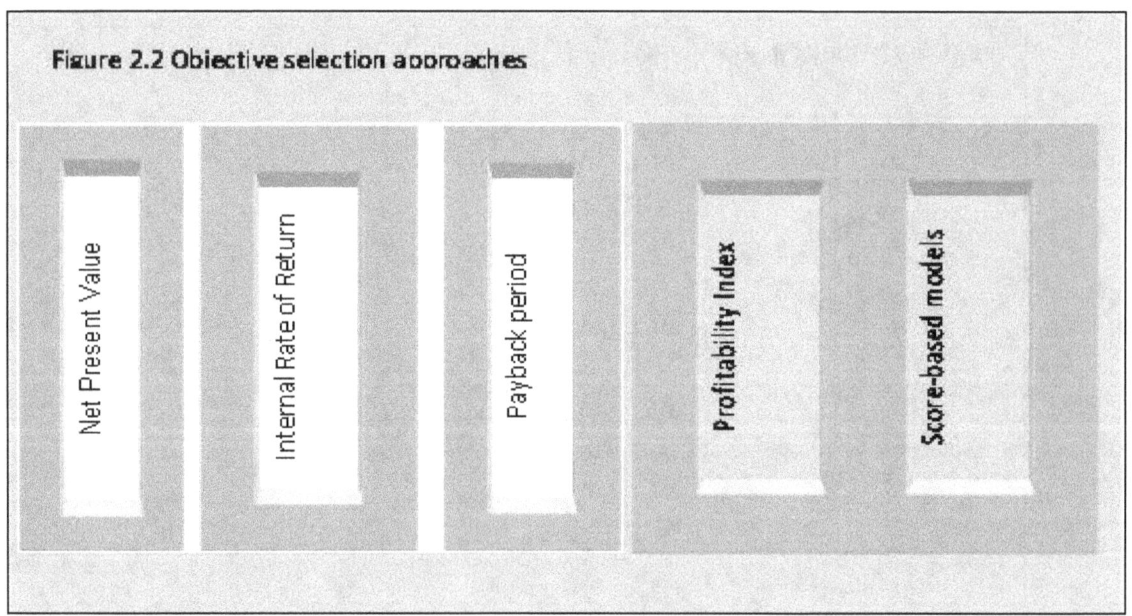

...

Table 2.2	Project choice with subjective factors
Subjective factors	**Score**
Capture market share	2
Customer satisfaction	3
Increasing company image	1
Fulfill social responsibility	2
Energy requirements	4
Comply with Government policy	2
Total	**14**

Project alignment with business strategy

Project alignment implies fitting project to the organization strategy and accommodating the project (a new initiative) in the current operations of the organization. It includes arrangement of financial resources, providing work force, extending support at different levels of organization and recognizing its importance at all levels of management (See Figure 2.3).

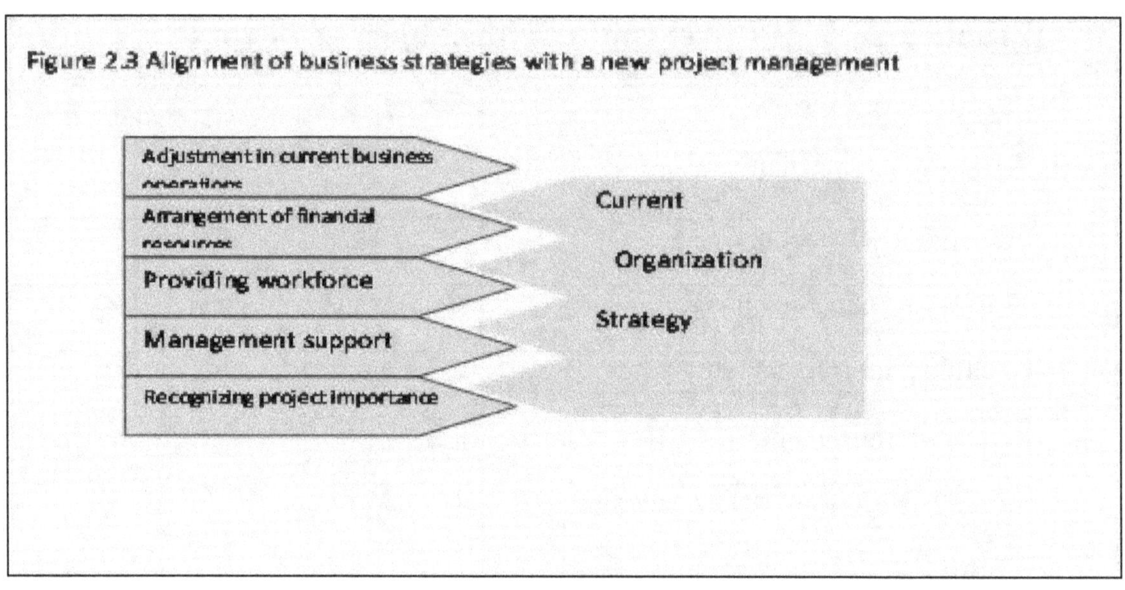

The second significant job of the entire project team is to adjust their project with rest of the organization and to develop project portfolio. Meredith and Mental (2010) offer several aspects to develop such a portfolio (See Table 2.3). Some of these factors are related with organizational activities and others are associated with project concerned or pool of other projects. The objective is to find out an optimal combination of projects; some of them offset dysfunctional effects of relatively week projects, but they are still included in the portfolio for the long-term benefits of the organization or they were "sacred cows", propose by senior managers / owners.

Table 2.3.	Factors for developing project portfolio
Steps	**Related element**
Step 1	Establish a project council
Step 2	Find project categories and criteria (contribution to organization's objectives)
Step 3	Collect project data (cost data, market benefits)
Step 4	Assess resource availability (both internal and external)
Step 5	Reduce (or rationalize) the project and criteria set

Step 6	Prioritize the projects within categories
Step 7	Select the projects to be funded and held in reserve
Step 8	Implement the process

Project portfolio shows the number of projects in operation and their contribution to the overall objectives of the organization. Table 2.4 depicts a hypothetical case of project portfolio. Profitability has been taken to reflect the impact of a project on the overall portfolio. Such comparisons can also be made for other factors to find a combined outcome to make the final decision.

Table 2.4   A hypothetical project portfolio

Projects	Contribution to organizational objectives
A	5% to profitability
B	6%
C	4%
D	5%
Average	**5%**

Project A and D are made according to the organizational requirements, but C is below it which is compensated with B. All the projects together achieve the organizational average which implies weak project (s) can be accommodated in the portfolio despite an individual project may not meet the criterion of acceptable.

Project initiation documents

Project Initiation Document (PID) is useful to define project and its scope, justify the project, a source of securing funding, defines roles and responsibilities of participants, provide information to the people involved to make them effective right from the start of the project (PMI, 2010). Project management institute supplies an indicative list of contents of PID for guidance; table 2.4 demonstrate them in a summarized version.

Table 2.4	Contents of project initiation documents (PID)
Sections	**Details**
Section 1 WHAT?	• Context of the project (background) • Project definition (purpose, objectives, scope, deliverables, constraints, and assumptions
Section 2 WHY?	• Business case (benefits, options, cost and time scale and cost / benefits analysis) • Risk analysis (risk identification, risk prevention, risk management and risk monitoring)
Section 3 WHO?	Roles and responsibilities (project organization chart / structure, project sponsor, project manager, project team)
Section 4 How and when	Initial project plan (assignments, schedules, human resources, project control and quality control)

In nutshell, PID "is a guide to a project, clearly laying out the justification for a project, what its objectives will be, and how the project will be organized. This helps ensure that everyone knows what is going on right from the outset." (ibid., p.4) It supplies the foundation on which the rest of the project can be laid down.

Review questions

1. Compare qualitative and quantitative project selection criteria.
2. Discuss the role of stakeholder (s) in selecting a project.
3. How current business operations are aligned with a new project?

4. Why a project portfolio is useful for a project manager?
5. Evaluate the need of project initiation documents (PIC) with an example of your choice (the project you like the most)
6. Project initiation is the first step in the life of a project. Explain.

3 PROJECT PLANNING

Learning objectives

Understand process of planning a project within a strategic plan

Explain components of project planning for a successful project.

Learn tools for planning a project in a portfolio of weak and strong projects.

Describe project planning techniques PERT and Gantt chart.

Introduction

Project planning defines the tangible and intangible resources with reference to time in various phases of a project. Managers estimate human, material, and auxiliary needs prior to launching a new endeavor to supply the right number of resources at the right time to ensure smooth progress of activities. It also persuades senior managers to remain committed to support the project and supply necessary financial resources; it is a tool to motivate other stakeholders to continue their support as well. Financiers arrange finance according to the project schedule such as working capital for different activities, milestones and unique events. Since borrowing money adds cost, therefore, timing and amount of monetary resources is important to keep the cost slice within acceptable limits. The manager of human resources deputes people for the new project; he hires, trains, and inducts added people to ensure the right number of skilled and unskilled employees are available at the right time. In addition, it involves an array of decisions on the part of operation manager, which are associated with project plan. Similarly, other participants need prompt information about project requirements so that they can plan their commitments as per plan. In short, the project plan offers guidance to stakeholders to get ready for the new venture in each time slot over the life cycle of a project.

Project planning

There are five planning tools for a project: project objectives, work-breakdown structure, project organization, project schedule, and project-performance baseline or budget (Johns, 1995) (See Figure 3.1).

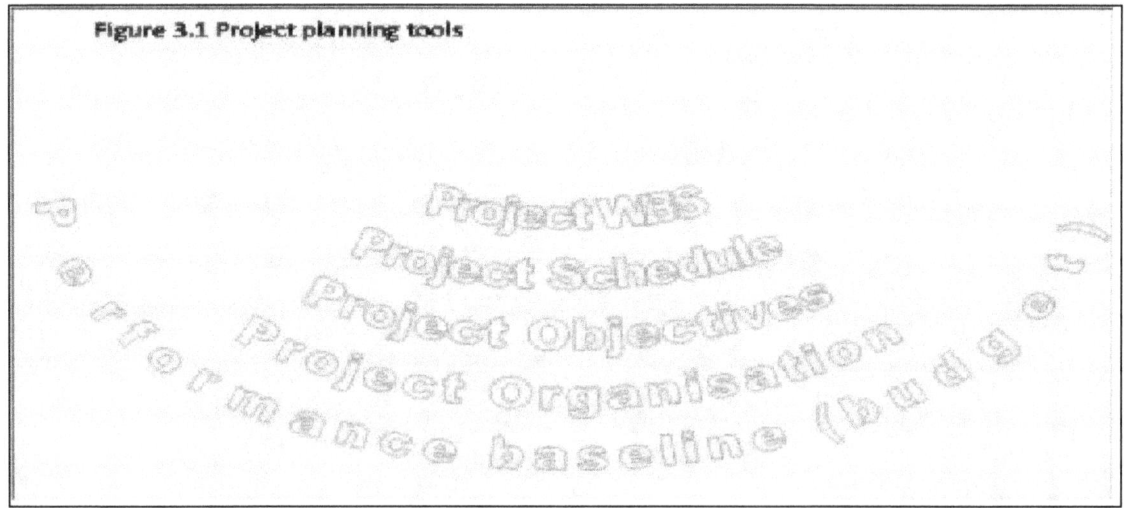

Zwikael et al, suggest another list for project planning,

> Project plan, project deliverables, W B S (Work Breakdown Structure) chart, project activities, PERT or Gantt chart, activity duration estimate, activity start and end dates, resources required for each activity , resource cost, time - phased budget, quality management plan, role and responsibility assignments, project staff assignments, communications management plan, risk management plan, and procurement management plan (Zwikael et al, 2005).

Project plans suggest things to be decided in advance "the sequence of activities required to carry out the project from start to completion" (Meredith and Mental, 2010). Plan should have project schedules, duration, physical / material resources, and human requirements. The plan also needs integration with the strategic plan of the organization and other projects in progress. In addition, Meredith and Mental (2010) believe a project plan should also include summary of the project, objective or scope, general approach, contractual aspects, risk management plan and evaluation methods (See Figure 3.2). This view needs more attention because it encompasses all the elements necessary for planning.

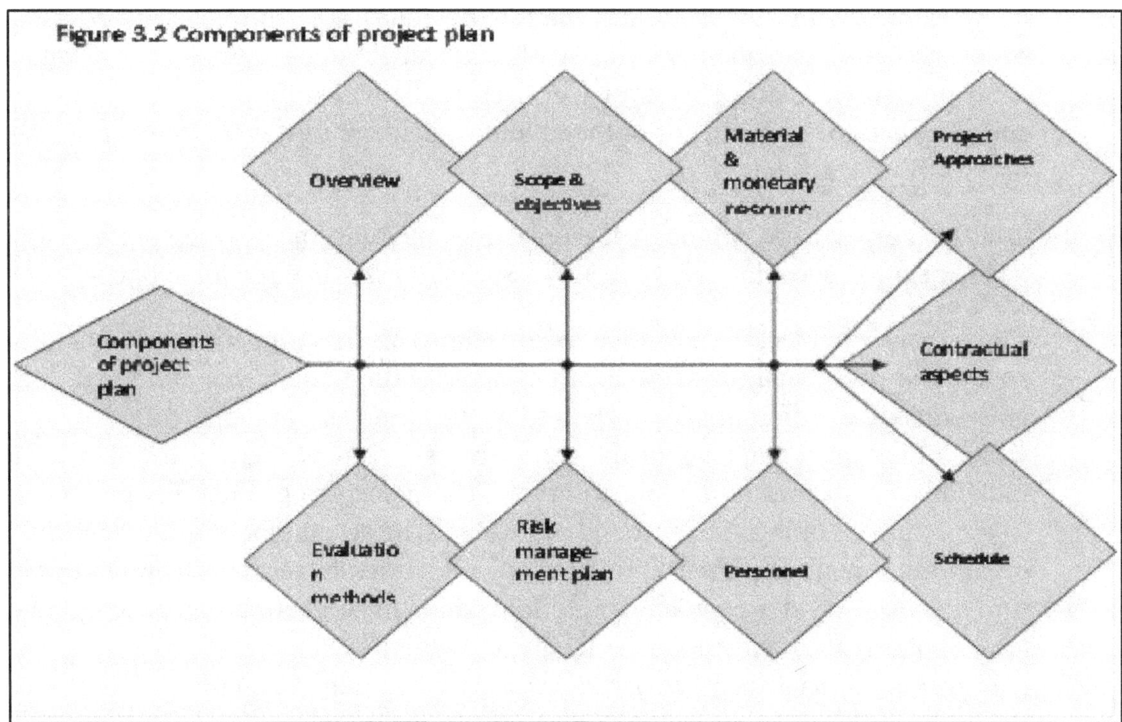

Overview of the project

It is a summarized statement of the key facts of the project involved directed to senior management to get buy-in or to continue to support it. It says the goal of the project and develops a relationship with objectives of the organization. For instance, senior managers decided in their strategic targets for the year 2011 that IT infrastructure will be modernized. This will trigger the introduction of the project (Replacement of IT infrastructure); the overview mentions it and says that the project is the realization of the strategic target set for the year. The overview describes the milestones and achievements / deliverables associated with them. For example, the project begins with advertising a tender in the press to receive the right number of bids followed by negotiation with potential supplier (s) for the purchasing of computers and related items. The negotiation also includes a schedule of delivery, installation, testing etc. The schedule delivery communicates critical steps involved in the project that may be a source of discussion for senior managers; the suppliers earmark the delivery dates; finance department get ready for payment and so on. The delivery-receiving department prepares itself for the expected deliveries and makes the necessary arrangement for it.

Objectives/scopes

The project needs demarcation of its boundaries from other projects especially when a joint venture is in operation and many companies are working on a project. British Aerospace (BAe) had a joint venture with four European partners for the development of EU2000 fighter plan. The entire project was divided into four components, each company had to complete one of them, under such circumstances, the part of the project or its part were given to 0.

each of the partners. Although the objectives of the project were common among the partners, other specific goals were also associated with the individual partners.

Three types of objectives are detailed in scope: profit, competitive aims and technical goals. The profit margin of each organization within their economic and competitive environment is different. For instance, in the BAe case, interest rate was different in various European countries in the recent recession, it affects the expense structure of individual companies in the joint venture. Therefore, the profitability targets were high in the countries of high interest and vice versa. The second factor is competitive aim; an organization may be placed under certain categories in terms of competitive position. Kotler (2002) divides companies into four kinds in marketing perspective but they are also applicable to projects management: leaders, challengers, followers and niche marketer or specialists in a particular area / segment of market. The leader of the industry would like to maintain its leadership through implementation of a certain project; for instance, a leader would like to replace old PCs with high specification machines or laptops because it might be the contributing factors for gaining competitiveness. On the other hand, a challenger may invest heavily in technology to get leadership in the industry. There are scores of examples of companies who have invested in research and development (R&D) projects to gain leadership. The most recent example is the Apple Inc. that had launched iPhone, iPod, and iPad because of investment in R&D projects. The company had gained substantial market share (21% in second quarter of 2010) because of these projects (Canalys, 2010). Obviously, to continue innovation and improvement of its existing products new projects, will be launched in the future. The third aspect is the specification of technical goals; the famous ISO standards are one dimension of it in addition to the terms of trade between the client (either internal or external) and the project management team. In software development projects it is known as user requirements, which is the first step for initiation of a project. Upon completion of software projects, the requirements are matched against product features (Box 3.1).

Box 3.1 Objectives of project scope

Profit
Technical goals
Competitive aims

Leadership of the market
Challenging leader
Following others
Specializing in a market segment

Material and monetary resources

We assume that a project has been found, its feasibility was conducted and the senior managers and other stakeholders were agreed to support and supply resources for the project. It may be worthwhile to mention that we are dealing with projects in organization as against projects for national level or public projects, which are normally aimed at improving life style of the people or maintaining it.

For illustrative purposes, let us assume that an educational institute is replacing / upgrading its old IT infrastructure: PCs, server, software, and books. It will be used as an example in the book.

When we think about resources, it refers to the monetary assets: capital expenditures and revenue expenditures. Capital expenditures are incurred on acquisition of tangible assets such as plant and machinery, delivery trucks, computers, and software. For example, refer to our computer up-gradation of an education institute, the money spent on buying new computers and putting them in functional condition are capital expenditures. It also includes expenses on transportation, installation, and insurance in the transit. In addition, if the said institute chooses to upgrade the existing computers by increasing their central processing unit (CPU), memory, hard disk, or any other part then the cost of their acquisition and installation are capital expenditure. The second category of expenditure is revenue expenditure; they are incurred on annual maintenance, wear and tear, electricity, and annual insurance or content insurance.

Project manager estimates both expenditures and document them. He coordinates with the finance department or external financing bodies to ensure availability of funds. Although it is not the area of project manager to buy financial resources, yet he must be aware of the process so that any lap in the availability of resources at a particular time during the life cycle of a project, can be adjusted accordingly.

Project approaches

This part of the plan deals with technical and managerial approaches applicable to the project. The technical approach describes the availability of technology to the project; whether the project is a brand-new endeavor or is an extension of one of the projects. For instance, Microsoft was upgrading its Windows and Office suite; the Windows was mere software which was run by other software e.g. Microsoft DOS (Disk Operating System) until 1995 when the first version of Windows operating system was introduced. It has been upgraded with later versions; we have Windows 7 now on the desktop. When Microsoft was extending Windows, the company knew that the technology was available to support their new or enhanced products. For instance, 256MB memory was enough for Windows 95, while Windows Vista required 1000 MB of memory to run it comfortably. Thus, the company assumes that the technology will be available when the new version of Windows will be launched on the market.

The managerial approach is related to control i.e., it ensures whether there is a deviation from the routine procedures. Weather the project completes with existing facilities / infrastructure or any subcontractors will be needed. e.g., using a new supplier for the supply of computers in the case of educational institute but separate contractor will be used for installation / testing.

Contractual aspects

It is one of the critical sub-sections of the plan which include a number of documents related with the project i.e., reporting requirements and their detail description. Meredith and Mental (2010) provide a list of those documents:

1- List and description of reporting requirements
2- Customer-supplied resources
3- Liaison arrangements
4- Advisory committees
5- Project review and cancellation procedures
6- Proprietary requirements
7- Any specific management agreement i.e., ., use of subcontractors
8- Technical deliverables and their specifications
9- Delivery schedule
10- Specific procedure for changing any of the above

Technically speaking it is the core of the plan that encompasses not only project elements but also provides the bases for the project organization, and control, the key subsequent phases in project management. For example, advisory committees reinforce the organization structure and reporting requirements lay down the foundation for monitoring and control.

Project schedules

Schedules are the eyes of a manager as the side mirror for a driver; he changes his strategy of driving a project on the bases of schedules; they play a pivotal role in the management of a project at each step of its life cycle. Schedules show activities, related resource availability, and any possibility of sharing resources with other projects. For example, the time of IT technician is shared for installation of software on the new machines in the upgrading IT infrastructure case. Since the technicians would perform their routine duties in addition to the replacement project, therefore, their time must be bought. Milestones and activity schedule are associated with time: beginning and ending dates, and relevant deliverable. Project schedule provides the road map for it.

Personnel

This section deals with human resource requirements; team formation, training, leadership and motivation are famous topics. Meredith and Mental (2010) described the following factors as a part of this subsection:

> 1- Number of people needed
> 2- Specific skills
> 3-Types of training needed
> 4- Possible recruitment issues
> 5- Legal or policy restrictions on workforce composition
> 6- Specific requirements such as security clearances

It is important to match human resource requirements with schedule and budget because they affect cost, which create long-term implications for the project. A time-phased strategy will be helpful to figure out how many personnel will be needed and when at various phases of the project or at various milestones. Coordination with the human resources department is helpful about these issues.

Risk management plan

Project risk is associated with both potential problems and unexpected benefits on the way to destination. It is a wise approach to expect them and make a contingency plan, if possible, to avoid their negative impacts on the project. Meredith and his colleague (2010) found a series of risks; it includes but is not limited to the whole spectrum. They are,

> 1- Default of subcontractor(s)
> 2- Unexpected technical breakthrough
> 3- Strikes
> 4- Natural disasters such as earthquakes, hurricanes etc.
> 5- New markets for our technology products
> 6- Tight deadlines and budgets

7- Sudden move by a competitor

Reiss (1992) believes that "a project is a high-risk project if a high proportion of activities have little or no float." Others believe crises and lucky breaks cannot be predicted, making a list of things "that can go wrong gets everyone in a negative state of mind. I want my people to be positive." (Meredith and Mental, 2010) They also refer Zawikael et al (2007) who found high-risk project can be managed better through project planning in four areas: schedule overrun, cost overrun, technical performance and customer satisfaction. Better project plans are an effective risk management approach than risk management tools, however.

Project evaluation methods

Projects are evaluated against their objectives, quality standards and triangular criteria: budget, delivery time and quality. Governmental agencies also demand a given standard to be followed in certain projects; project planners are required to obtain such guidelines and incorporate them in the plan. Evaluation helps to assess a project for monitoring and controlling purpose; it also provides learning for subsequent projects in the organization.

Project planning techniques

An effective way to plan and control projects is to use network techniques such as Gantt chart and Programme Evaluation and Review Technique (PERT).

Gantt chart

Gantt charts were introduced during first half of the previous century; the exact date con not be determined due to many views of researchers. Some believe it was the work of H L Gantt, other hold an opposite opinion; it was the joint innovation of F W Taylor (The author of Principles of Scientific Management) and Gantt's work of 1903 or it was based upon the work of Taylor. Irrespective of its start, the planning technique is known with the name of H L Gantt. It was meant to plan and manage batch production, a production-planning tool. In contemporary terms, Gantt chart was a time-phased demand dependent planning approach where end-time requirements were linked with constituent components. The purpose was to ensure availability of the components and tracking them later. These were used to plan production on a daily basis by determining the quantities to be manufactured. It became the basis of tracking production against goals. (Wilson, 2003). Gantt called it balance sheet as quoted by Wilson (2003), planning and control involves two sets of balances: what an employee was supposed to do and what has been done. And the amount of work to be done and has been done. This was considered the foundation of contemporary Gantt chart. Wilson states "It identifies the items to be produced, the number to be done each day and in total; and the date when production was to start and finish." (ibid., p. 431)

The theory of graphic presentation is useful for comprehensive plan for the entire factory. It implies the job order or sales driven organizations can apply it in addition to project management. Gantt chart is a powerful planning tool for developing project schedules; they are simple and are constructed easy even in complex projects. Each task with its duration is depicted on it. Activities are shown on y-axes and time on the x-axes. The size of the horizontal bar figures out the length of time involved in a given activity. The thickness of a bar may show the number of resources a particular activity needs or consumes in monetary terms although other parameters can also be depicted. Figure 3.4 shows a simple Gantt chart which assumes that each activity consumes an equal number of resources.

Figure 3.4 Gantt chart with equal number of resources

Activities	Planning						
			Execution				
					Control		
1	2	3	4	5	6	7	
Timeline							

The above chart shows a sequential arrangement of three activities in the project where each activity consumes equal number of resources and the dependencies are simple i.e., execution starts when planning completes. Nevertheless, the activities may be started at the same time and work in parallel to each other (Figure 3.5).

Activities	Activity A					
		Activity B				
					Activity C	
1	2	3	4	5	6	7
			Time periods			

The chart can be expanded by including the amount or quantities of resources that each activity is consuming. Figure 3.6 shows both dimensions if activity Planning takes 25% of the total resources, Execution 50% and Control 25%. Execution consumes twice as much resource as planning and control do individually. The height of the bar illustrates the number of resources being taken by a certain activity.

Activities and their resources							
	Planning	(25%)					
			Execution	(50%)			
					Control	(25%)	
1	2	3	4	5	6	7	
			Timeline				

The chart can also show the milestones and constituent activities. Two activities are shown in Figure 2.7 for the sake of simplicity.

	1	2	3	4	5
Activities and their resources		Milestone 1 [Resources (25%)]			
			Milestone 2 [Resources 50%]		
				Milestone 3 [Resources (25%)]	
	1	2	3	4	5
	Time periods and milestones and their constituent activities				

...

Figure 3.8 Gantt chart with varied number of resources, milestones and their activities

Activities and their resources	A1	A2		
	Milestone 1 [Resources (25%)]			

1	2	3	4	5
		Milestone 2 [Resources 50%]		
			A5	A6
A3		A4		
			Milestone 3 [Resources (25%)]	
1	2	3	4	5
Time periods and milestones and their constituent activities				

A1-A6 denotes activities in the milestones, an enhancement in the earlier figure.

Another addition is possible in the chart by dividing the resources into more than one category. Figure 3.9 illustrates three types of resources employed in each milestone.

Resources are assigned to each task, which is commonly known as work breakdown structure (WBS). Figure 3.6 – 3.9 show some examples of WBS. In addition, major activities are shown hierarchically into successive levels where each level becomes a finer representation of successive levels.

The "Gantt chart graphically displays the work breakdown, total duration needed to complete the tasks, the resources allocated as well as percentage completion of the project" (Kumar, 2005). The chart is helpful in project planning, developing planning schedules and controlling project costs. Kumar (2005) provides details of how to plan, schedule and control costs in his recent work.

Gantt chart is the most effective tools used in practice (Conforto and Amaral , 2010). Murphy and Ledwhit's (2007) survey of 96 high-tech SMEs in the Republic of Ireland found nine project management tools and techniques: project teams (20) , project planning (19), Microsoft project (16), Gantt chart (14), change control processes (10), project control (8), critical path methods (4), stage gate process (4) and earned value management (1). The figures in brackets are the number of companies responded /

reported. Fifteen percent of them are using Gantt chart for planning and controlling their projects. Two project-planning techniques were reported: Microsoft Project and Gantt chart. Fifty-three percent of them apply for Microsoft Project while 47% use the Gantt chart for project planning. Conforto and Amaral (2010) refer a study conducted by Maylor (2001) which reports that transnational companies use Gantt chart for planning and control of their projects.

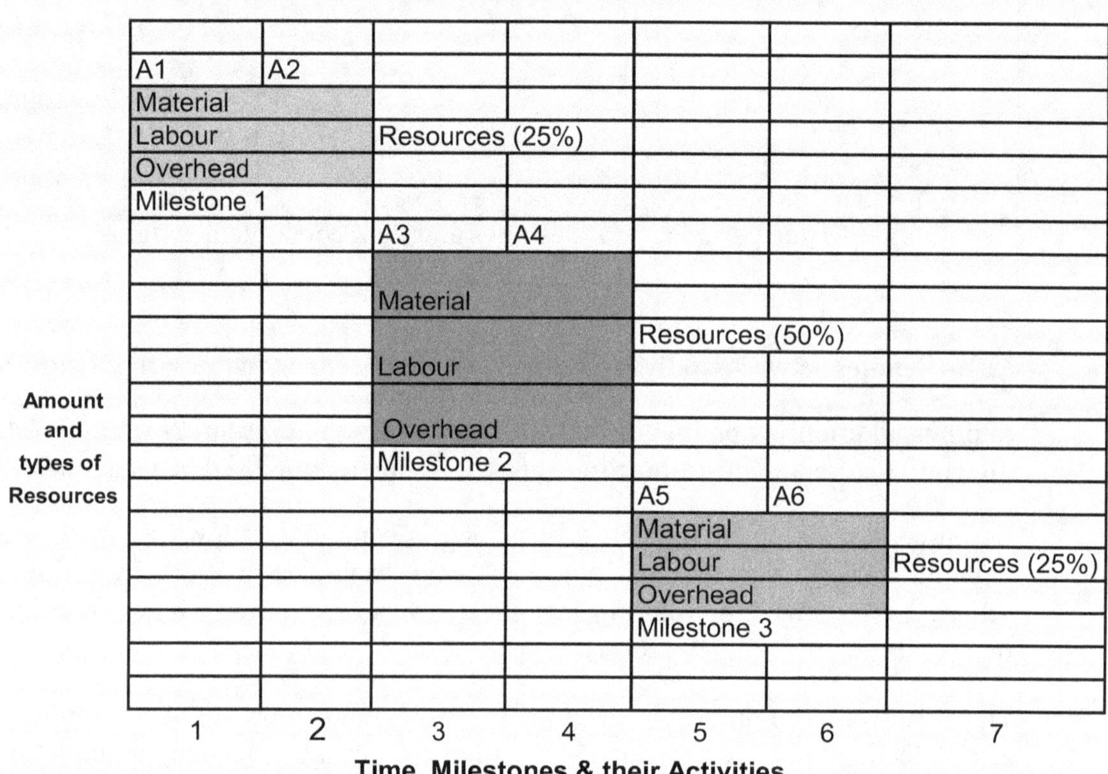

Figure 3.9 Gantt chart with milestones, activities within a milestone and varying amount of resources

Programme Evaluation and Review Techniques (PERT)

The technique along with critical path method (CPM) is widely used in project planning and control (Omer, 2009). He believes that the most recent project planning and controlling software is based upon the PERT / CMP philosophy. The PERT process consists of eight steps: breaking down the project into activities, determining how activities are related with one another, identifying the sequence in which activities should be carried out, constructing a network of activities and events reflecting their relationships, estimating the time for each activity, identifying critical path (s), re-planning the network by shifting interchangeable resources from non-critical to critical activities in order to minimize the project completion time, and using the network , as developed and finalized to monitor plan implementation during the life of the project (Kuklan, 1993). Table 3.1 is a redefined part of these steps (Kuklan, 1993)

Table 3.1	Represents a redefined parts of PERT
Components	**Steps**
Activities	1-3
Network	4
Estimating time	5
Finding critical path	6
Redefining resources	7
Implementation and control	8

Finding activities for a project

The first three steps are related to activities, the basis of developing a network that is a pictorial reflection of activities with dependencies. For instance, suppose there are ten activities in a project (for illustrated purpose) which can be denoted as A-J. One way to depict them may look like the one shown in Figure 3.10. It is not helpful to the project manager or other people involved because it reflects activities sequentially. However, it may be meaningful if it is converted to a project network (Figure 3.11).

The diagram depicts the concept of a network. Activities a & f begin together which implies resources are needed for both simultaneously. Similarly, b and g can be started upon completion of a and f. Since two activities are starting at the same time, therefore, less time will be needed to complete the project, at least 50% less time as compared to the figure 3.10. However, activities do not always start and finish in the way as shown in figure 3.11; projects are much more complex in practice than the one shown here which need more complicated and efficient solutions. Project managers address the issue through network analysis and development. We have found a network for understanding the issue in the following lines.

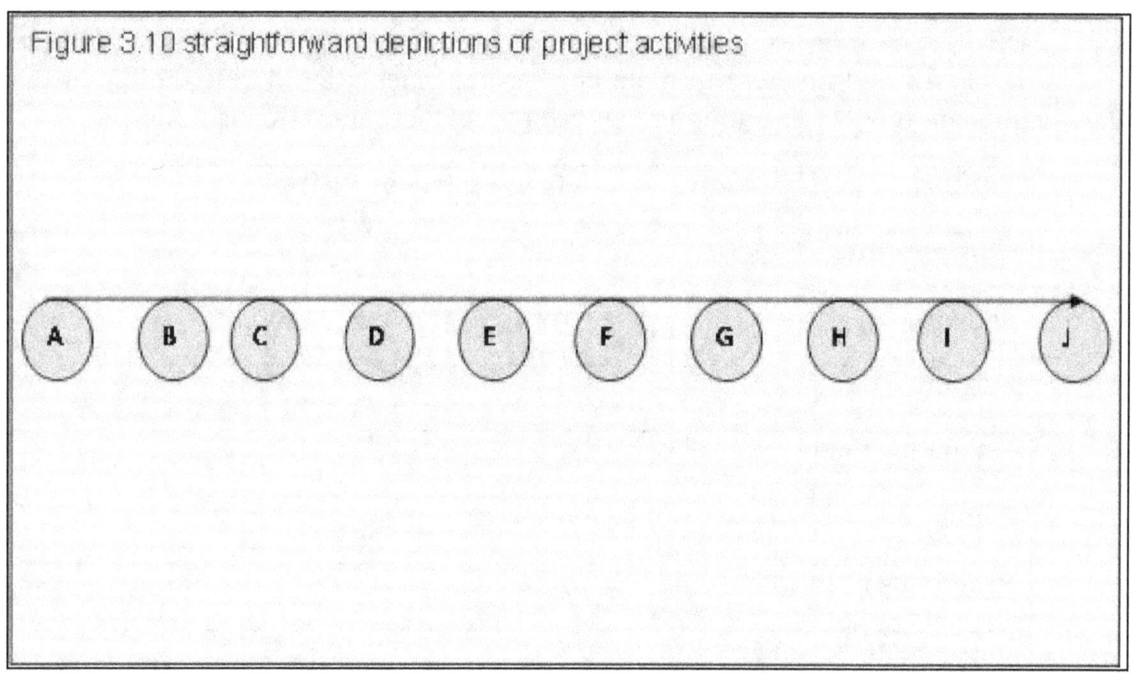

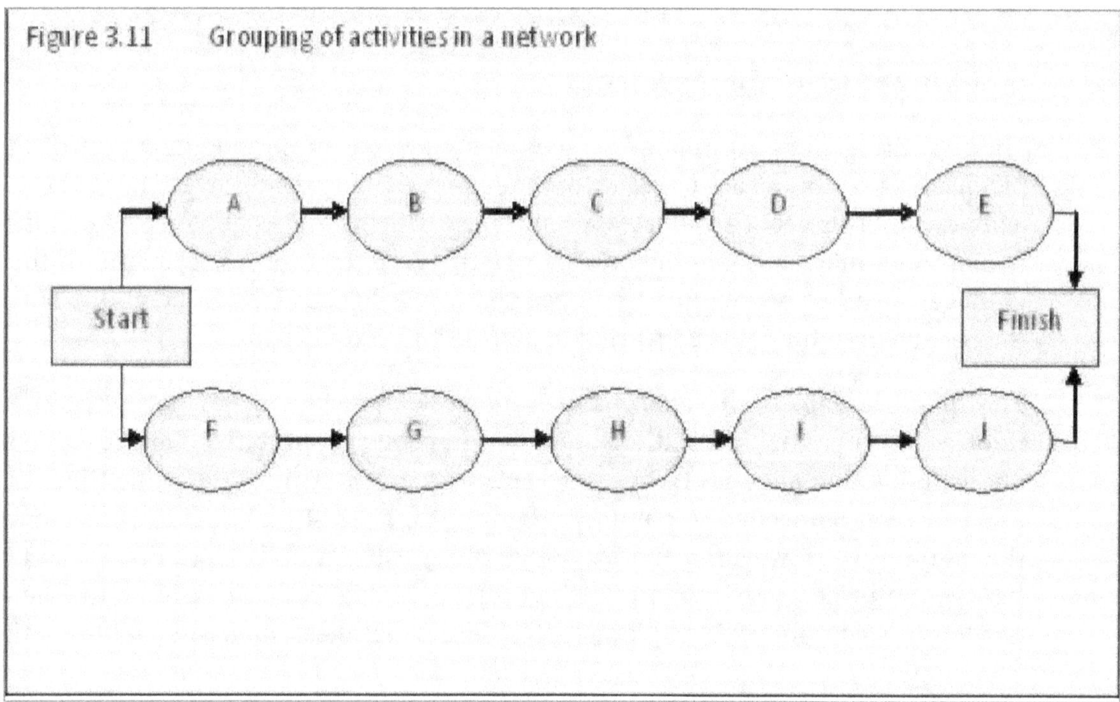

Table 3.2 Estimated duration of activities			
Activity	Duration	Activity	Duration
A	3	F	2
B	2	G	3
C	5	H	9
D	3	I	4
E	6	J	3

Estimation of activity timing

The next task is to estimate the timings of each activity (See Table 3.2)

Creation of dependencies

Table 3.3 shows the dependencies of various activities.

Table 3.3 Dependencies of activities			
Activity	Following activity	Activity	Following activity
A	E	F	G
B	E	G	H
C	E	H	J
D	I	I	H
E	D, F	J	None

Finding the critical path

Estimation of timing of activities and dependencies of activities enable us to find out critical path. Figure 3.12 shows a network and the critical path of the project

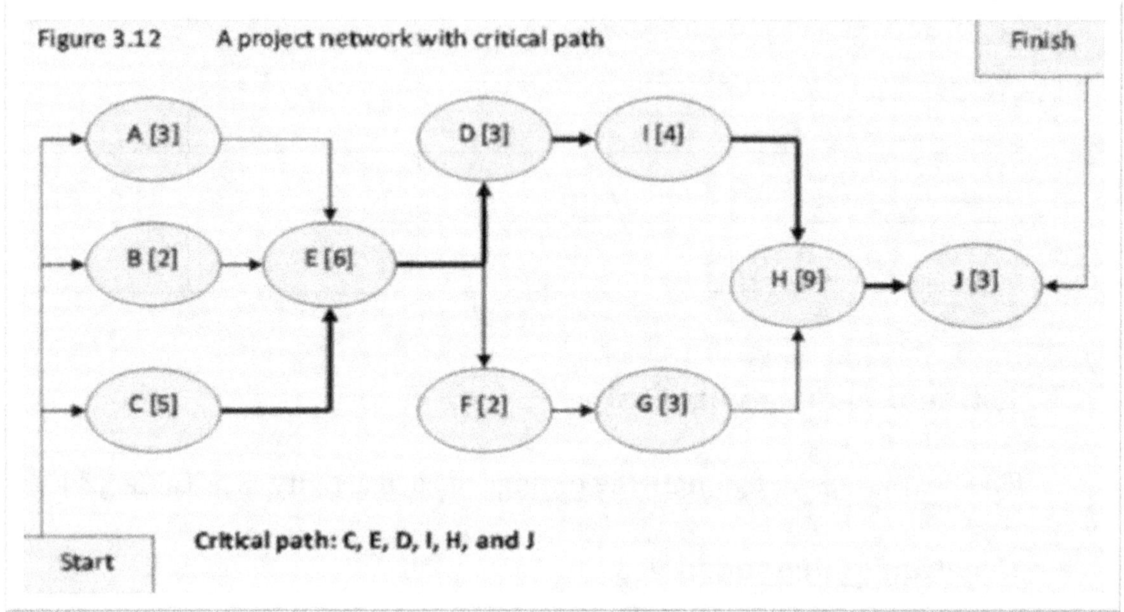

based-upon table 3.3.

The duration of CP is 30 weeks, the only longest path in the project (See Table 3.4).

Table 3.4 The duration of critical path	
Activities	**Duration**
C+E	5
E+D	6
D+I	3

I+H	4
H+J	9
J+FINISH	3
TOTAL	30 WEEKS

Analysis of the network

The total duration of the CP is the greatest among the available alternatives. Table 3.5 shows other possible alternative and their duration.

Table 3.5   Analysis of another available alternative

Option A		Option B		Option C		Option D	
Activities	Duration (Weeks)	Activities	Duration (Weeks)	Activities	Duration (Weeks)	Activities	Duration (Weeks)
A+E	3	B+E	2	B+E	2	A+E	3
E+F	6	E+F	6	E+D	6	E+D	6
F+G	2	F+G	2	D+I	3	D+I	3
G+H	3	G+H	3	I+H	4	I+H	4
H+J	9	H+J	9	H+J	9	H+J	9
J+FINIS	3	J+FINISH	3	J+FINISH	3	J+FINISH	3

H								
TOTAL	26	TOTAL	25	TOTAL	27	TOTAL		28

Although the critical path is the longest of alternatives, yet it is the most efficient way to complete a project because it saves total project time by 10 weeks while incorporating all activities. Finally, all the activities included in the CP are critical activities.

The next task is to distribute resources to each of the activities according to their requirements. Allocation is possible on the basis of many factors; some managers allocate resources on the bases of time slot each activity consumes. The rationale for such allocation is that if an activity remains in progress, it uses resources (See Table 3.6).

Table 3.6   Analysis of time taken by each activity

Activity	Time (Weeks)	Percentage time
A	3	7.5
B	2	5.0
C	5	12.5
D	3	7.5
E	6	15.0
F	2	5.0

G	3	7.5
H	9	22.5
I	4	10.0
J	3	7.5

Allocation of resources

Suppose the total budget for the project is £150m, the amount of budget for each of the activities based on the percentage is shown in table 3.7.

Table 3.7 Allocation of resources based on percentage of time consumed

Activity	Percentage time	Budget (Millions of Pounds)
A	7.5	11.25
B	5.0	7.5
C	12.5	18.75
D	7.5	11.25
E	15.0	22.50
F	5.0	7.50
G	7.5	11.25

H	22.5	33.75
I	10.0	15.0
J	7.5	11.25
Totals	**100**	**150.0**

The network or PERT structures a project, saves time and resources, provides peace of mind to the people involved and materialize the expectations of an organization. The project life cycle is followed in an efficient way and projects are easy to manage.

Project organizing and control is the subject of the next two chapters. There is a famous 'management phrase' that planning looks ahead and control looks back. The next chapter chalks out the bases of looking back.

Review questions

1. Critically evaluate project planning process

2. Why is it necessary to understand components of project planning?

3. Differentiate between components and tools of planning a project.

4. Compare planning techniques PERT and Gantt chart; which is better and why?

5. Evaluate PERT as a network strategy.

6. Critically evaluate Gantt chart as a diagrammatic technique for depicting milestone or activities and time involved.

4 PROJECT ORGANIZATION & RESOURCE ALLOCATION

Learning objectives

- Understand how to organize a project in teams and units

- Explain allocation of human, non-human resources including techniques of allocation of activities

- Learn tools for allocation of resources and activities or milestones.

- Discuss the need of teams in managing projects and the way they are managed

- Know how to select a productive team

- Learn the qualities of a project leader.

Introduction

Smith (2007) defines organizing in a generic perspective, he says "organizing is the process of determining who will perform the tasks needed to achieve organizational objectives, the resources to be used by the way the tasks will be managed and coordinated." There are at least three elements stemming from the above statement: figuring out and assigning tasks, allocation of resources, and deciding management and coordination of both tasks and resources. We will take them in turn in the following lines.

Distribution of project tasks and activities

A project is usually a part of a programme and a project has activities and tasks. For instance, a university offers many educational programmes, say an MBA; there are many modules in the degree: marketing, finance, IT, management, and others. Each of which is a project for a student. Under the semester system, a student must sit mid and final exams; these can be termed as activities. The same student attends a series of lectures, workshops, seminars, and tutorials, which can be classed as tasks. Sometimes tasks and activities are used interchangeably; Smith's argument supports this view; he implies tasks instead of activities; this book adopts his view and implies tasks (as described in the definition) as activities for the sake of simplicity.

The tasks and activities are distributed on a full-time or part-time basis. Part time arrangements are called integration where "project tasks are executed along with daily work. Project members remain at their desks working in the normal environment." (Anderson et al, 1995). This arrangement is beneficial because the entire organization stays at the disposal of the project manager that can be used for the betterment of the project. It also provides flexibility in that the project manager can find suitable people for related tasks, it is easy for him to fit worker to the job and job to the worker. A larger number of people can be involved in the project than a fixed number of team members. The project is considered the responsibility of organization (See the case study CMP for an empirical exemplar of the strategy), therefore, project members maintain their expertise. Integration creates coordination between project team members and other people (outside the scope of a project). Project members share their problems and progress with other colleagues, which increases involvement, a strategy generally used for motivation and boosting productivity. It also enables both organization and project managers to use resources more effectively; many resources such as printers are shared while forming a separate team needs separate printer, for example (See Figure 4.1).

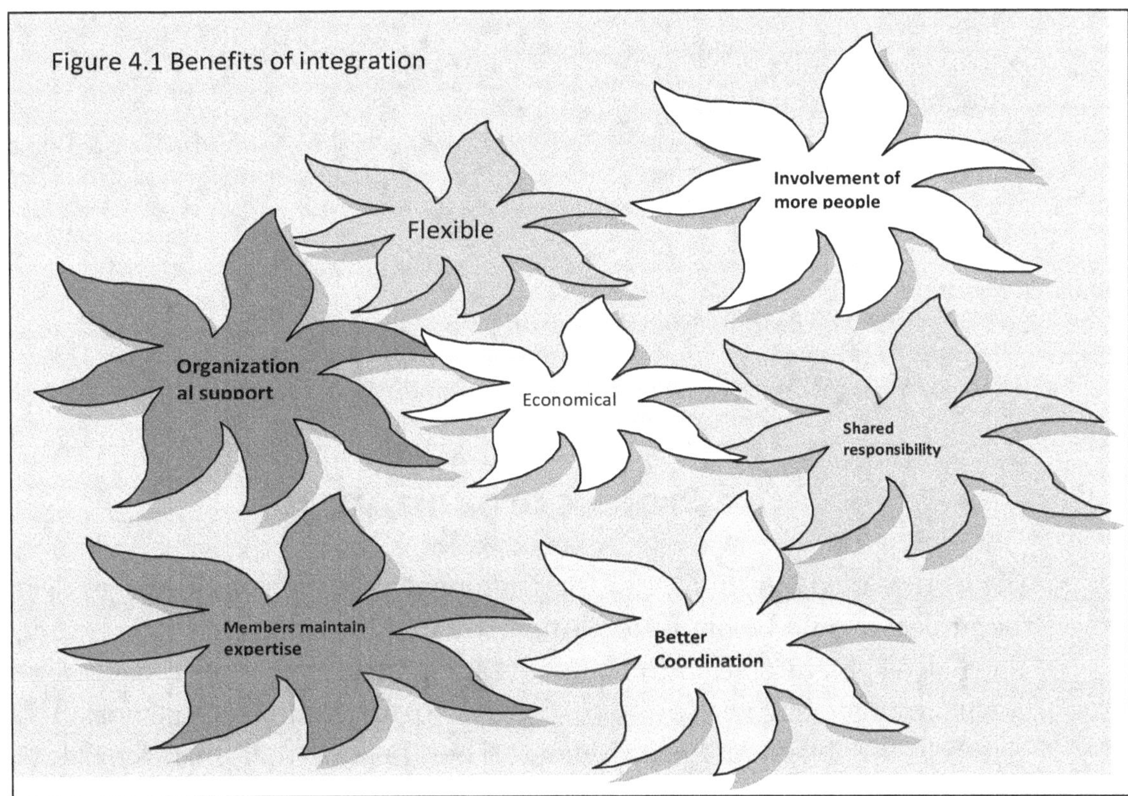

The other alternative available to project manager is to release project members from their daily work and move them in a project room where they work on the project. Under such arrangements, the project team concentrates on a project without external interference and disturbance. However, there are number of concerns about independent project teams. The team does not receive support of other people outside the scope of the project and the project manager may create "state within the state". It becomes easy for him to create a group and gain power, which may last even after the completion of the project. The thinking of the project team is restricted within the project and their ability is no longer available to the organization. This way is also notorious for poor use of resources especially when some decisions are supposed to be taken by the base organization or senior managers (Box 4.1).

Box 4.1 Pros and cons of independent project teams

Pros
Focus on the project
No interference or disturbance

Cons
Less support from outside the scope of the project
Individual influence of project manager
Politics and power play in the project
Team ability no longer available to base organization
Poor use of resources
Slow decision making especially when senior managers are involved in it

Project organization

The next related question prior to assignment of responsibilities is to decide how the project should be organized. Anderson and his colleagues (1995) suggest two alternatives: hierarchical arrangements and matrix structure. The former is a top-down arrangement where junior reports to the immediate senior; it makes a hierarchy or layers of management. They believe that hierarchical structure creates hierarchy or layers of management. They believe that hierarchical structure creates bureaucracy, inefficiency, poor use of resources, outside people in the organization show little commitment for the project and lack of informal contact between the project and its surroundings. Nevertheless, hierarchical structure has some benefits as well: describes the responsibilities of various organizational units, shows chain of command etc. The hierarchical arrangement partly depends upon the nature of organization and its culture (See Figure 4.2).

The second available alternative is matrix organization: it is famous for flexibility. Anderson et al (1995) state that it is helpful for better decision-making, enhanced communication, flexible organization, best use of resources, better adjusted to people and problems. According to them, "in matrix organizations groups and individuals are arranged in various constellations of responsibility and authority depending on the matter involved." Matrix structure is useful for multi-product and or geographically dispersed organizations where a product or regional manager heads each product or region. He manages the region as a division where a separate hierarchy exists in the region to concentrate on the geographical area. Similarly, a product manager is still responsible for his product, marketing strategy, customer relationship strategy, promotional strategy and sometimes its financial strategy. However, it misses the merits of hierarchical structure (Box 4.2).

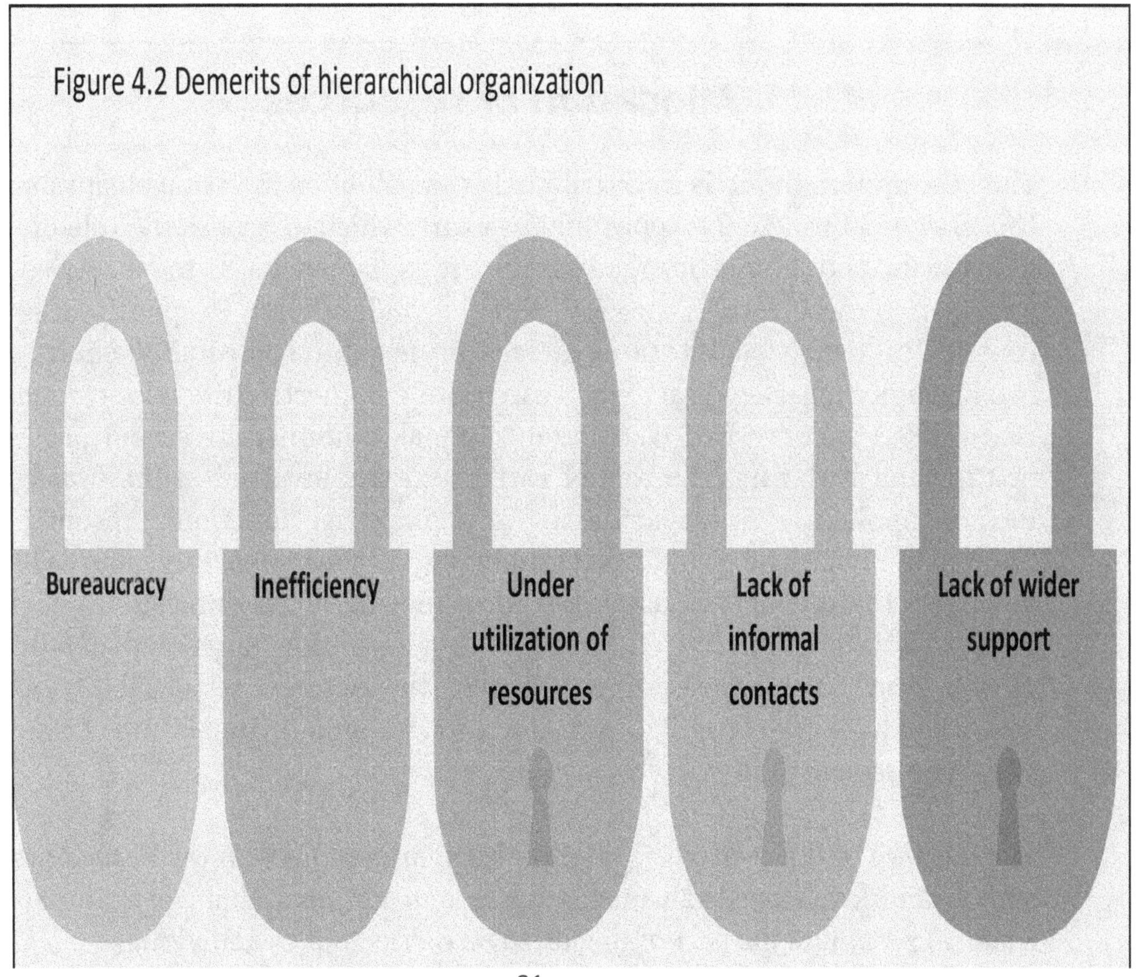

Although there are more demerits of matrix organization, its merits out weight them. Which implies it is a suitable alternative for project managers.

Box 4.2 Features of matrix organization

Argument in support
Flexible
Better decision-making
One-to-many communication
Economy of resources
Adjustable to people and problem
Argument against
Unable to claim benefits of hierarchical structure

Allocation of resources

The next important job is to distribute responsibilities to various team members. It is assigned through a responsibilities chart, which describes the role of various individuals, and groups or organizations. It explains what is to be carried out by who i.e., project owner, project director and others. Responsibilities chart consists of details about three areas: principal responsibility chart, project responsibility chart and activity responsibility chart. Principle responsibility chart (PRC) is concerned with organizational, administrative, and professional matters and it clarifies the role of various parties involved in the project work. PRC is applicable in departments or managerial functions, resource types (human, monetary etc.) and work groups. Project responsibility charts (Pro. RC) highlights the role of various parties for achieving project milestones as defined by the project team. Pro. RC is also developed for functional departments, groups, and types of resources. Finally, the activity responsibility chart is concerned with project activities to concentrates on individuals and clarifies their role (Anderson et al 1995).

The purpose of these charts is to organize a large project on the bases of role and responsibilities rather than on the bases of traditional chain of command. The chart (s) pinpoints the part of the job to be carried out by individuals, groups and organizations and fix the responsibilities of the concerned (Box 4.3).

Box 4.3 Charts and their purpose

Kinds of charts
Principle responsibility chart
Project responsibility charts

Purpose
Organize a project on the bases of roles and responsibilities
Fixes responsibilities

Responsibility chart has task reference, task name, and the responsibility of the relevant person. It also shows the nature of the responsibility: primary or supporting. Figure 3.3 shows a sample responsibility chart.

The chart can be developed for functional departments, cost centers or even divisions (SBU). Similarly, activity charts can be prepared in the same way assign individual, groups, or organization level activities. Responsibility is preceded by authority, which in turn creates accountability.

Figure 3.3   Sample responsibility chart

Task reference	Task name	Person1	Person 2	Person 3
T1	Gathering information	☐	◯	
T2	Developing model	◯	☐	

T3	Testing model			

= Primary responsibility
= Supporting responsibility

Managing resources

When projects are completed, they become resources of an organization or nation; software is developed for keeping details of employees, students in a college, patients in a hospital. However, prior to completion it consumes a lot of resources: caliber of people, plants, machinery, computers, cash, raw material and so on. This section is devoted to a brief discussion of resource allocation.

Reiss states five steps of resource management: defining, distributing, aggregating, leveling, and smoothing (Reiss, 1992). Let us take them in turn.

Resource definition

Defining resources involves forecasting the probable list of resources. For a construction project, it may include number of engineers, masons, carpenters, laborers, steel fixers, joiners, electricians, painters, supervisors, and others. The construction projects consume cement, bricks, wood, windows, doors, steel bars, and electrical material to name a few. Moreover, the most precious resource, the time; how many days, weeks, months, or men-hours will be needed. Project manager or his team would estimate each of these according to project specification based on their experience; industry parameters or standards are also helpful indicator. Computer software is used at this stage to estimate by hit and trial method. A reasonable list is produced because overestimate increases cost and underestimates increase the possibility of being out of stock. In addition, pessimistic and optimistic scenarios for each of the resources are also developed.

Allocate resources

The next task is to distribute resources; it implies each task is linked with one or two resources, which have been identified in the previous phase. The resources are allocated on the bases of duration of each activity and work content or workload. Project manager takes each task and allocate resources to them. For example, in CMP case study, cutting whole chicken is a task, the manager assigned four cutters or personnel to it. Since they share other resources, such as cutting worktop, knives, cutting machine etc., therefore, they are not specifically allocated to them. Table 4.1 shows allocation of personnel and other resources to each task defined in CPM case study.

Table 4.1	Allocation of resources to various tasks			
	Resources			
Task	No. of personnel	Worktop	Cutting machine	Cutlery
Whole chicken	4	Shared (all can use it at the same time)	Shared (one can use it at a time)	Shared (used individually)
Boneless breast	2	"	"	"
Drumsticks	2	"	"	"
Mince	2	"	"	"
Chicken wings	2	"	"	"

e tasks was equal because the project was to complete within a specified time depending upon the time available to the responsible persons. Sometimes, as Reiss (1995) argues that a particular resource may be needed disproportionately: a particular task may need four personnel in the first week, two in the second week, three in the following and so on. In this case the project manager must create a resource demand profile that should demonstrate the demand of resource over the life of a project.

Resource aggregation

Although total resources are calculated manually for small projects but is a time-consuming job for large projects. The purpose is to arrive at the total amount of resources required for each task on a daily or weekly basis. Project management software makes the job easy and provides aggregate resources needed for each task for the desired duration. It helps to compare resource availability and resource demand, a key function of planning and controlling projects and its resources. Project manager can also make "make or buy" decision for certain resources. For example, in construction projects, earth morning machinery is normally hired for daily or hourly basis, contracts may be signed for demand of such machinery with hiring companies so that machine would be available as required on the specified time to make the operations smooth.

Resource leveling

Resource leveling is a software function and PC generated report saying the match of resources available and required. Reiss (1995) states that the resource leveling is, "a process by which the software ensures that the project never demands more resources than you have available." Although the software makes things simple by matching available and required resources, it delays the project because it takes the task in sequence i.e., the tasks entered in the earlier dates receive resources first. The later tasks are automatically delayed; therefore, some important tasks may be postponed. It requires prioritization of tasks and creation of dependencies to ensure smooth movement of project in the right direction on the part of manager. It is possible manually in small projects but it may create some idle resources. If such resources belong to the organization, as in the case of our case study CMP, then extra resources can be used for day-to-day work. Even if they are idle, they do not increase project cost because they have not specially bought or hired for the project. However, in small organizations where resources are hired on a limited basis; the idle resources increase cost.

Resource smoothing

The last step in resource management is resource smoothing. According to Reiss (1992), it involves smoothing out "the jagged peaks a trough of the two grams to improve resources utilization ... by adjusting the timing of activities within their float, by moving resources from activity to activity, and by many other techniques such as sub-contracting and prefabrication." Manual alternative may be more efficient than mechanistic solution.

Reiss (1992) suggests some strategies to make it more productive: subcontract some resources i.e., hire, take some tasks out of critical path and do them earlier, shift resources from tasks to task and check through your logic i.e., re-examine your assumption about dependencies. In addition, find out alternative ways to execute project, and think how the project plan can be improved in a project team meeting (See Figure 4.4).

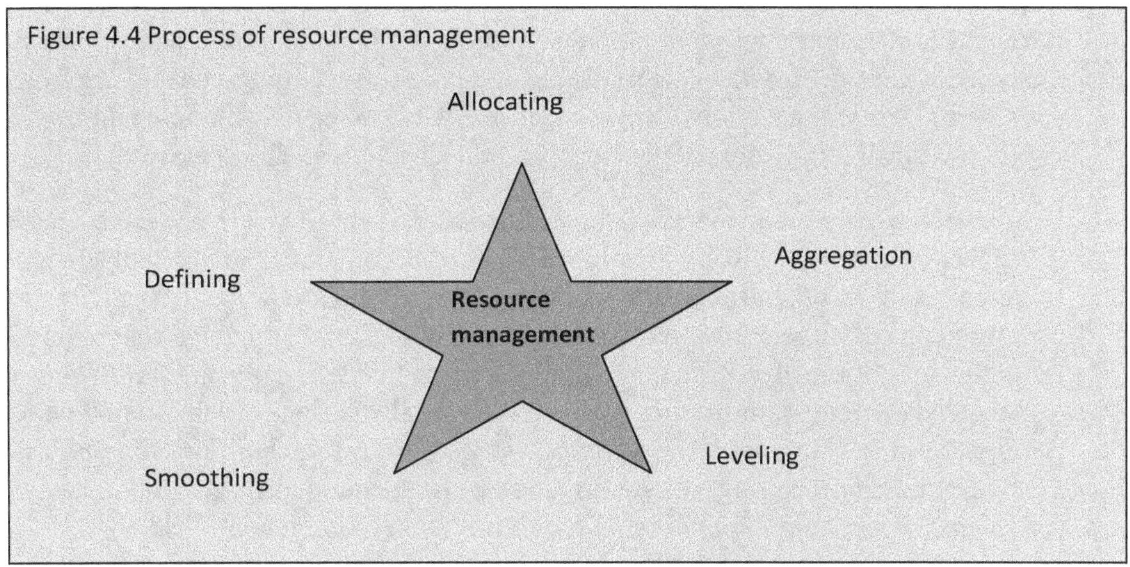

Teams in projects

A team is a group of people chosen for carrying out a task, activity and or a project. The team members are selected with the assumption that they are capable, competent, and willing to work for a specific job. Earlier experience is not necessary for the endeavor, but it may be an advantage. The choice is made by the immediate head or by a senior manager and participation can be volunteered to ensure willingness of potential members. Managers apply objective or subjective analysis techniques to check the suitability of potential member. Personal relations, likes / dislikes or other factors lead managers to include a particular person in his team. For instance, a member may be a "sacred cow" selected and suggested by a senior member of management team. Objective analysis is made on account of previous experience on similar projects, qualifications, special skills, willingness to join the project and other factors.

A prudent project manager selects right people and keeps them motivated to remain loyal to the project over its life cycle. Project members also need periodic training to get afresh with the changing demands of the job. These elements are examined in the fourth paragraph.

Team selection

One of the most important decisions a project manager must make, for the success of a project, is to select the right people. It implies fitting members to the team and team to the member. Two questions are important in this regard: project manager / senior manager or a combination of both select the team members keeping in mind either the subjective or the objective factors. Some employees are volunteered and are free to join a team in large organizations. However, it might not be applicable in small organizations where a small number of people work, and the question of choice may not be possible.

Manager selects team members on the bases of subjective or objective analysis. The subjective approach involves choice of team or any member under four circumstances. People work in organizations in formal ways and informal ways. Informally groups are formed on social, religious, economic, and regional bases. Language also plays a key role in the formation of informal groups. When people are associated with any of these perspectives, they want to work with their informal colleagues in the formal team i.e., the project teams. It implies if the selector belongs to an informal group, she / he chooses his colleagues from among the group. Senior managers also get influenced by such circumstances; therefore, the selectors honor their recommendations.

Apart from personal relations, project manager or senior manager may like the way of working of a person (s) and wants to include him in the team. Again, he picks up the person subjectively. Organizational politics also play some role in the selection since the organization are groups of like mined people who cooperate on matters, they like and support the person they happy with. There is no exception for project manager; he needs political support and must include one or more members in his team; in other words, he must inject some political blood in the project team.

A professional manager does not select team members purely on the relationship grounds, they also evaluate them on objective factors. It begins with the collection of data about potential candidates. The parameters for choice range from project management qualification (certification of PMI) to willingness to take part in a particular project. Earlier performance on working on similar projects is considered an added advantage. Specific requirements or skills such as engineers in construction projects and system analysts in software management projects are classic examples. The overall capability is measured by developing a table to obtain a cumulative score that can be a source of selection decision (See Table 4.2).

Table 4.2	Skills of a team member
Objective	**Subjective**
Specific skills	Likes/dislikes
Performance	Political reasons
Experience	Sacred crow
Qualifications	Personal relations
Willingness	Affiliation with a social group

Each factor needs recognition according to its importance in the selection decision and relevancy for the project. For instance, a score or numerical value is assigned to each of the elements listed in table 4.3. Table 4.3 shows the hypothetical values assigned on the scale of 1-5 in a software project, where 1 is the minimum and 5 being the maximum.

Table 4.3	Allocation of hypothetical scores to a software project	
Factors	**Relevancy**	**Score**
Specific skills	Degree in IT	5
Performance	Earlier assignments	2
Experience	On the similar projects	3
Qualifications	Membership of professional body	4
Willingness	Agree to work	5
Total		19 (76%)

The candidates with the highest score will be recommended/selected. Bennis and Ward (1997) talked about great groups / teams. They have found key features of a great team such as the ability to work together and the sense of teaming. These features stem from inheritance, training, social circumstances, experience, education and so on.

Team motivation

Motivation keeps the members in the team until the job finishes. People are inspired by monetary, non-monetary incentives and fringe benefits. There are many non-monetary benefits offered in the employment world. The behavior of manager and immediate supervisor plays a decisive role because employees are   knowledgeable and enjoy choice of work.   A manager must be a leader who should have certain features in order to motivate members so that team remains a productive machine for the project. Research shows that people like to be recognized, respected, and helped at odd times. Table 4.4 depicts some of the recent findings about the way employees want to be treated.

Table 4.4	Features of a team leader for motivating its members
Area	**Related factors**
Leader related	1. Recognize individual contribution of members 2. Each challenge must be seen as a possibility and opportunity 3. Focus on individual strengths and develop them 4. Removing obstacles as a superhero 5. Improve the performers 6. Work as a part of team rather than its 'boss' 7. Acknowledge people's contribution regularly 8. Be the model of accountability 9. Show progress and communicate it to everyone
Organisational related	Generate clear achievable goals with a reasonable approach

The outcome would come as a collective effort, a spirit every manager wants to inculcate in an effective team; great teams believe they are 'on a mission from god'. Well, a great idea on its own, deputation from the creator; it implies such teams will be self-controlled because they feel they are accountable to Him. It makes people great, great people form great teams, and the great teams do great jobs.

Review questions

1. Briefly describe the project organization process.

2. Evaluate the criteria for allocation of non-human resources to a project.

3. Compare various charts used for allocation of responsibilities of team members.

4. Compare full time and part time (integration) approaches to carry out an endeavor

5. Differentiate between hierarchical and matrix organization techniques.

6. Describe in detail the resource allocation process.

7. Objective skills are enough for a team member. Explain.

8. Using Table 4.4, develop a similar table for a construction engineer who is to work at an airport.

9. How is a software engineer's job different from a construction engineer?

10. Why a project manager should be a leader rather than a "manager"?

5 PROJECT MONITORING AND CONTROL

Learning Objectives

- Understand control as applicable to project management.

- Learn the process of controlling projects.

- Know progress reporting mechanism.

- Explain project control strategy and controlling techniques.

- Describe project success factors and the reasons of project failure

Introduction

When resources are allocated, and responsibilities are assigned the relevant team (s) implement their part of the work. Project manager and others oversee various aspects of paper plan into tangible products with the passage of time. They receive reports about the progress and match them with envisioned or planned version of the project; they take controlling actions (if necessary); this phase is known as monitoring and controlling. This chapter examines key aspects of the phase to ensure that the project is heading towards the right direction.

In addition to the above, Meredith and Mental (2010) suggest cost controlling and monitoring procedures to keep things in control. Procedures must be in place to control cost/budget at proper levels; milestone is one of the examples to examine reports and take any measure if necessary. Alternatively, periodic method can be adopted as Anderson and his colleagues have suggested a fortnightly review of project activities and taking controlling action as needed. They believe that control must be in place even if no variance is found (Anderson et al, 1995). Greg states controlling project encompass configuration management, change control management, performance reporting, procurement management, requirements management, issue management, risk management and quality management (Greg, 2008).

Monitoring is related with controlling; Reiss (1992) suggests two techniques for meaningful monitoring: do it yourself (DIY) and other people's effort (OPE). The former means to involve the project management team in the process by visiting project site (office, special rooms etc.). For example, for computer procurement projects, the project manager pays visit to the officer in charge of buying the equipment. The purpose is to investigate what the progress of the project is. Whether the computers are manufactured, are in transit, have arrived and need installation etc. It creates a relationship and enhances communication among team members, becoming a source of motivation. Satisfactory progress of the project develops a sense of accomplishment and in case the project is not on track, the new targets can be set.

Efforts of other people suggest examining the progress as perceived or compiled by others, a traditional strategy of monitoring. A better way to address the issue is the combination of both approaches to corroborate what is going on.

Project control

Project Management Institute (PMI, 2004) defines controlling as, the controlling processes are those processes that ensure that project objectives are met by monitoring and measuring progress regularly to identify variances from plan so that corrective action can be taken, if necessary.

There are certain key messages in the statement: control is a process (s) of measuring and monitoring progress regularly, the process finds variances, take corrective action for achieving project objectives. The process starts with monitoring of the progress and translating it into quantitative terms so that magnitude of deviation can be determined. The focus of this effort is to meet objectives of the project in particular and achieve organizational objectives in general. It is an ongoing process and managers start it from the inception of a project.

The above process sounds good; however, Greg (2008) questions it on the ground that it ignores prevention. He suggests a three-step model to address this issue: prevention, detection, and action. He assumes 'prevention is better than cure'; according to him *prevention* is the best way to keep your project on track is to prevent (or at least minimize) variances from occurring. How do you do this? This takes your entire array of project management skills, but a few key activities include investing in planning, communicating effectively, monitoring risk factors continuously, resolving issues aggressively, and delegating work clearly.

Prevention begins with project planning; the previous chapter describes the planning process. Although it seems a pathological solution, nevertheless, it is the only way that leads towards successful completion of a project.

The next step is to *detect* variances; Greg (2008) conceptualizes it as "for this aspect of project control, think "radar system" or "early warning system"; project control should provide early detection of variances. The sooner we can act on a variance, the more likely we are to get the success factor back on track". It needs a mechanism in place, for him,

> The key for early detection is to have the tracking systems and work processes in place that allow for the prompt measurement of project results. Common examples of detection methods are performance reporting and review meetings. Two important concepts to note here are that to have a variance, you must be comparing actual results to a baseline of some type, and a variance can apply to any of the critical success factors including stakeholders' expectations and quality, not just schedule, cost, and scope.

Once variances are identified, they should be eliminated or minimized to avoid snowball effects on rest of the project.

The third element in the Greg's (2008) triangle is *action*. He believes that   it must include, "three most common action … corrective actions, change control procedures, and lessons learned. Often, as part of the planning for project control, specific variance thresholds are established that dictate what variances and corrective actions can be managed by the project team and what ones need the immediate attention of senior level management." Action is needed where variances are identified; Andersen and his colleague (1995) state, the control process must be in place even if no variances are found. Preventive strategy can minimize the probability of occurrence but cannot end the possibility of variances (See Figure 5.1).

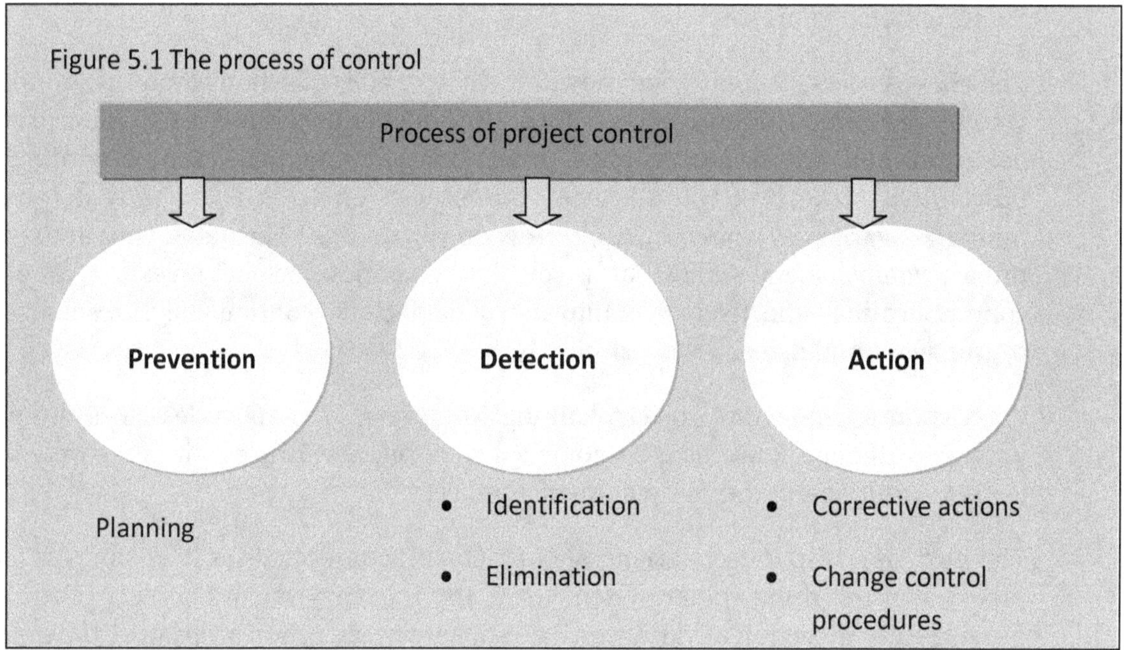

Given that let us see an alternative view of project control; control is based upon measurement of progress against plan; if things are not going as intended than measures must be taken to bring them in par with the envisioned parameters. For Anderson et al (1995) control is a managerial activity; it "involves analyzing the situation, deciding what to do … presuppose that a certain amount of paperwork be done." In case of any discrepancy project or milestone objectives are changed (e.g., delivery time, cost etc.), bringing in more resources to meet the deadlines / schedule, rearrangement of workload, and changing dates of milestones.

Control Fundamentals

A reporting mechanism, criteria, documentation required, and communication procedure and tools are key components of control. They are being taken in turn in the following paragraphs.

Reporting mechanism

Andersen et al (1995) believe control cannot work without an effective reporting mechanism in place, establishing control criteria, coordination of plan and reporting. Effective reports apply predetermine templates or patterns for reporting progress. Both good news and sad news should be included in the reports; some project managers believe only good news is not enough, bad news should be included as well to reflect both dimensions of the phenomenon.   Reporting not only show performance but also is a source of motivation and psychological encouragement to the entire project team. Formal paper-based or electronic reports and team discussions about performance are highly recommended. It brings out the individual feeling of success. Secondly, the experts recommend visible actions to recognize the individual and group input received from teams.

Reporting criteria

The second element deals with the *criteria* of reporting; project manager decides to review essential matters in advance including cost, quality, and schedule. However, other criteria depend upon the nature of the project concerned. Sometimes the choice of manager plays a decisive role in the definition and selection of "critical success factors" at various stages or milestones.

Documentation

Another key principle is reporting on the plans; according to Anderson et al (1995) "reporting should occur on a document which also shows the actual plan. Each time a report is made, it must subsequently be compared with the plan." It ensures keeping the report to the point. Sufficient room should be provided on the plan for this purpose and multiple copies must be made to support the idea. It is important to send deviation / variance reports to those who have authority to take corrective actions or enable them to take some step to do so.

Communicating reports

Finally, reports must be sent at a fixed *interval*; monthly reporting is appropriate at milestone level while fortnightly reporting is usually suitable at activity level. Some managers prefer to report when a milestone is achieved. Rozenes et al (2004) found characteristics of a strong control mechanism in construction projects: ongoing managerial efforts to achieving project objectives, allocation of appropriate amount of financial resources, work break down structure must be established hierarchically, project team should be monitored at the work package level. Most essential element is the ongoing managerial behavior; some managers believe that control is a periodical job. Examining reports at fixed intervals or milestones is the most effective way; if something goes wrong than corrective measures should be taken at once. The approach has been criticized on the ground that it multiplies a minor problem into an issue that may need significant resources and may affect other activities and milestones. Nevertheless, some managers believe a continuous control system is much more effective than the periodic one where corrective action are taken without waiting for a specific periodic report (Box 5.1).

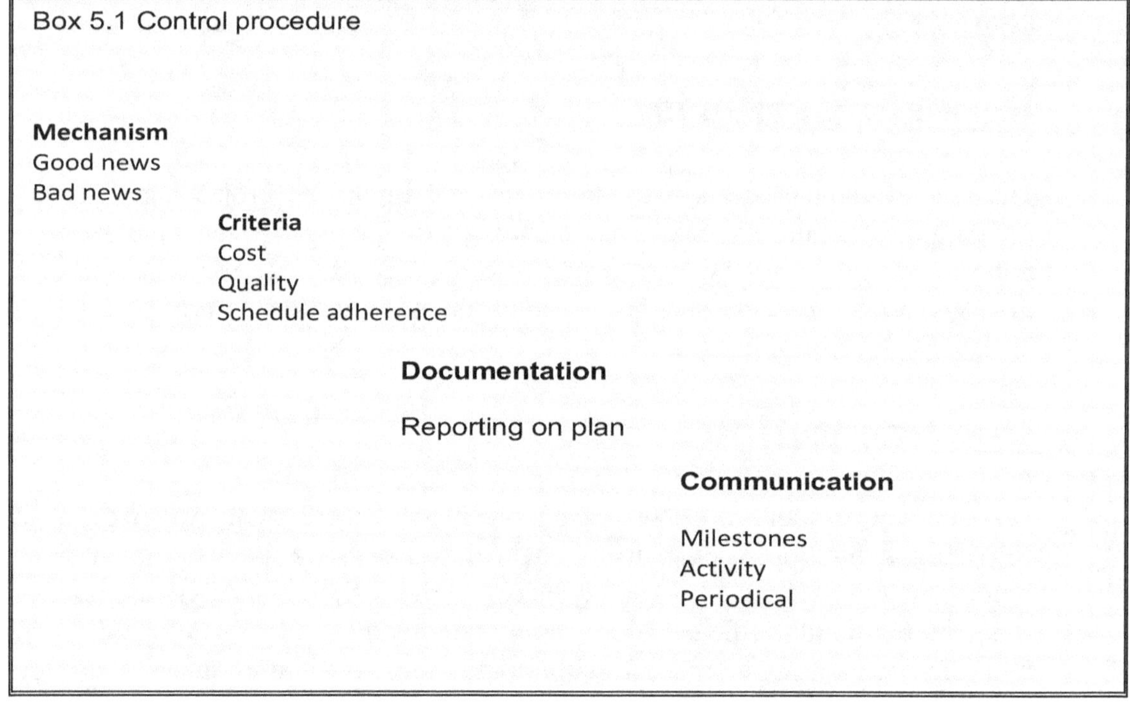

Project control techniques

Tradition methods of project control is associated with historical data which predict the possible variations in future. They do not consider unforeseen events or "situations they are surprising or develop outside the scope of project plan" (Nikander and Eloranta, 2001). They also argue that these methods ignore human and cultural issues.

Cost-based

Cost-based reporting or simply cost reporting is well known and common in practice. Under the system, the actual cost is matched with planned figures and a variance is calculated. Any positive discrepancy is highlighted, and cost control measures are taken if it overruns the planned figures. It also forecasts the total cost of the project due to changes in the cost structure or trend to date. Nikander and Eloranta (2001) questioned it on1` the grounds that it focuses on only cost-related matters.

Project scope management

Rozenes et al (2004) describe some more techniques: project scope management (PCM) addresses specific issues to achieve "other" project aims. The PCM defines procedures to alter project content to motivate stakeholders, increase knowledge base, accommodates technological developments, and changes in project process. Another tool is called design review (DR) which involves "a series of design reviews (DR) which typically contains predefined control points through a project life cycle." (ibid., p.110).

External parameters

There are some external control parameters, which are the responsibility of base organization since they are the part of supply chain management and, therefore, considered out of area of an individual project manager. The base organization deals with them on an ongoing basis rather than for a particular project through five Rs: right quantity, right quality, the right price, the right supplier and the right time and place. (Andersen et al, 1995)

Miscellaneous

There are other methods available for examining project performance: bar chart schedule, schedule performance, work performance, the earned value methods, and cost/schedule control system criteria. They focus on project events, an objective analysis of event (s). Nikander and Eloranda (2001) argue that these techniques are useful if used with critical path method.

Saladis (2003) argues the importance of control, he says, "controls should be established for all projects regardless of size. Without control, projects can become wild very quickly and in many cases, trying to regain control becomes an enormous and costly effort." He suggests a series of actions for it; Table 4.1 shows them in a categorical form.

Table 4.1	**Project control strategy**
Category	**Details**
Establishment of control processes	<ul><li>Establish mutually agreed upon monitoring and control processes at the start of the project</li><li>Develop and communicate a change control process.</li><li>Clearly define an escalation process and follow it</li><li>Separate personal interests from business issues</li></ul>
Team functions	<ul><li>Create a change control team and assign a change control manager</li><li>Use the ability of the team for plan development and to find solutions to problems</li></ul>
Communication	<ul><li>Communicate the importance of "Freeze Dates" and the consequences of not seeing them</li><li>Communication with the sponsor or project executive helps keep things under control</li></ul>
Create ownership	<ul><li>Ensure that all issues and action items have owners</li></ul>
Expect realistically	<ul><li>Set expectations early. Set them intentionally</li><li>Revisit expectations on a regular basis to ensure they are still valid. Reset when necessary</li></ul>

Steadfastness	Do not keep changing your mind. You can quickly de-position yourself and lose credibility

Project success factors

Although the idea of CSFs was originally coined for management of an organization, yet it is equally applicable to project management. Critical factors play a key role in the success of a project, missing any of these may lead to failure or not achieving envisioned objectives. Rozenes et al (2004) report some of them: clarity of goals, management support, ownership, a control mechanism, and communication. Soderlund (2004) adds clear project plans and client relationship; however, "the traditional triple constraint criteria seam to prevail." (ibid., p. 189). Greg (2005) provides a detailed list of such factors, table 4.2 classify them in a new form.

Table 4.2 Critical success factors for a project	
Category	Relevant factor
Organizational	• Project is aligned with organizational goals • Project has effective management support. • Proper investment must be made in planning
Stakeholder oriented	• All key stakeholders are in agreement on the purpose, goals, and objectives of the project • All key stakeholders share a common vision on the project results. • All key stakeholders share *realistic* expectations for the project results. • Each stakeholder and team member's role(s) and responsibilities are clearly communicated and understood
Technical	• The project results meet the expectations of the key stakeholders. • Stakeholder expectations are constantly managed and validated throughout the project • The project scope, approach, and deliverables are clearly

	defined and agreed upon during planning • Each stakeholder and team member's role(s) and responsibilities are clearly communicated and understood • A high priority is placed on correct and complete work effort estimates • A realistic schedule is developed and agreed upon • The project team has a strong results-focus and customer-orientation. • Project communications are consistent, effective, and focused on "understanding" • Project progress is measured consistently from the current baseline • Project issues and subsequent action items are aggressively pursued • There is a powerful sense of collaboration and teamwork. • Expectations and changes surrounding scope, quality, schedule, and cost are actively managed • Human resources are skilled and available when needed. • Project team proactively finds risk and determines mitigation strategies to reduce project exposure. • Project team predicts and overcomes obstacles to ensure project meets objectives.
Managerial	• Project should have effective leadership.

The organizational elements are those for which the entire organization is responsible. For example, investment in planning processes, which is done at strategic level. Since more than one project may be in progress at any given time, the alignment of each of them with organizational objectives is essential to acknowledge the existence of each of the projects. It also motivates the project team in that they are being honored for their contribution. Finally, the support of senior managers is a key factor in any of the planned change initiative and project management has no exception.

Furthermore, Greg (2005) summarizes characteristics of a successful project: all the deliverables are delivered as stated, it is completed as per schedule, the project does not overrun the envisioned budget, the project meets all the functional and quality specifications, achieves its objectives, goals and purposes, meets expectations of key stakeholders and clients, and maintains win-win relationship. He says win-win relationships implies "the needs of the project are met with a "people focus" and do not require sacrificing the needs of individual team members or vendors. Participants on successful projects should be enthusiastic when the project is complete and eager to repeat a similar experience." It suggests that the project team and key stakeholders including clients should define and agree success criteria prior to commencement of a project.

Reasons of project failure

Projects failure rate varies from 28.5% to 57.3% due to many reasons in software field as reported by Ambler (2008). Hameri (1997) states some of them: ignorance of what other project teams are doing; lack of discipline in design change control; diverse views on what are the objectives of the project; rigid project planning and scheduling routines; poor reactivity to sudden changes in the project environment; and unforeseen technological difficulties.

The generic criterion for unsuccessful project is not meeting triple constraints: not completing on time with budget and not meeting quality standards. In addition, Azzopardi (2010) reports a detailed account of reasons for failure of projects:

(a) Lack of a valid business case justifying the project

(b) Objectives not properly defined and agreed

(c) Lack of communication and stakeholder management

(d) Outcomes and/or benefits not properly defined in measurable terms

(e) Lack of quality control

(f) Poor estimation of duration and cost

(g) Inadequate definition and acceptance of roles (governance)

(h) Insufficient planning and coordination of resources

Most of these are causes occur at the planning stage except c and e. For example, if objectives (achievements) are not defined and agreed with stakeholders, the project team cannot visualize what to achieve. Everyone will be working in his / her own direction or employees will define their own objectives. Project objectives provide target (s) which define tasks and activities; wrong objectives lead to wrong tasks and activities. It leads to a waste of time and efforts in both defining and performing activities and tasks. In other words, absence of right objectives could lead to failure.

Review questions

1. Planning looks forward and control looks back. Explain.

2. Process control consists of prevention, detection and action. Explain them with suitable examples.

3. Briefly describe the fundamentals of project control.

4. Compare various project control techniques.

5. Evaluate cost-based control approach in service industry.

6. Project control strategy consists of six dimensions; briefly describe them.

7. There are at least four groups of projects success factors. Stakeholder oriented is one of them. How stakeholders make a project successful?

8. Azzopardi (2010) put forward eight reasons for project failure. Do you agree with him? If not, what are the alternative factors of project failure.

6 MANAGING RISK IN PROJECTS

Learning objectives

- To know the nature of risk
- Find out the sources of risk in projects
- Understand the way to control risk in projects

Risk in Project

Risk is the uncertainty associated with desired outcome; variation in the inputs (material, money, human resource, and time) of a project. "Project uncertainty is the probability that the objective function will not reach its planned target value". (Jaaffari, 2001). Objective functions are compared with project variables: cost, quantities of input resources and external factors etc. Risk management is the process of identification of risk, assessment of their impact management's action to control them and providing for residual risk in project estimates (Perry, 1986). So, risk management is a set of actions to be taken at various stages of a project life cycle. Risk identification and assessment of its impacts are carried out prior to initiation based upon experience or scientific tools and techniques available. Management's actions to control them are performed both prior to and during the execution. For instance, some actions are taken to reduce the consequences. Ensuring supply of raw material or components from more than one supply reduces the probability of being out of stock. Secondly, unavoidable risks are transferred to other parties such as insurance companies; insurance policy is bought prior to launching and the cost is included in the total cost. Some actions are taken during the execution, a control function manager does as a part of managing projects. It makes measuring performance regularity, matching with planned parameters and taking corrective actions, if necessary. Finally risk management involves providing residual estimates risks; it is the unavoidable component of risk to a part of the project that adds up to cost of project and is bearable by the organization concerned.

Key question is how the risk is found and assessed to minimize its impact on the project. Frank (1987) suggests a risk analysis and assessment model; his thesis is based on two premises: risk structure (uncertainties within project) and risk classification (quantitative and qualitative). Quantitative can be measured in hard figures i.e., the budget will overrun by £50,000 the delivery time will be 10 weeks later than the planned time framework.

Perry (1986) identified a number of sources of risk as classified in Table 6.1 with reference to construction projects.

Table 6.1   Sources of risk

Category	Risk source
External factors	External stakeholders such as clients, regulatory agencies, government Exchange rates Inflation Funding and fiscal issues Construction contractors Logistics and plant supply
Internal factors	Estimating data Construction material (usage) Construction labour (application) Project organization Project definition Construction equipment
Discrete sources (Design)	Adequacy to meet need Experience or competency of design company Degree of novelty Appropriateness of design Realism of demand on construction and design programme Likelihood of design change

Frank (1987) provides a checklist of risk or sources of it, it includes risks associated with quantities and efficiencies, resulting from dependencies (customer, supplier and others), uncertainties as to payments, uncertainties as to liabilities (delay, penalty etc.), warranty risk and scheduling risks.

Frank also suggests risk analysis and assessment techniques. The risk identified from the sources listed above can be forwarded by classifying various risks and their impact. One of these techniques is known as ABC classification; the risks are classified as grade 'A' (the high impact), B grade (the minimum impact). The same writer suggests Delphi technique for assessing risk, the procedure of Delphi for the assessment include formation of representative expert teams who assess qualitative risks. They provide cost assessment of project risk. The experts should be provided exact definitions of various risks to delineate from one another. The cost assessment is tabulated, and a profile is drawn in graphical form. It must show ABC classification along with total risk.

The next logical step is to define a risk management strategy. Baldry (1998) suggests a four-dimension risk management strategy: risk retention, risk reduction, risk transfer and risk avoidance. Risk retention involves bearing unavoidable risk. For instance, in public sector organization economic loss is sustained by the organization itself even though they do not offer or support any insurance cover. However, disruption risks arising from postponement, cancelation or non-performance of projects are retainable. Commercial organizations reduce their risk by distribution of financial risk over other parties such as subcontractors. Such organizations transfer risk to professional organizations that are born to bear risks i.e., the insurance companies. The strategy to deal with risk is to avoid it; in certain situations, the risky projects are scrapped at first stage of feasibility study.

Project life cycle and risk

Ward and Chapman (1995) argue management of risk during various phases of project life cycle (PLC). They name it process risk; their thesis is about control of risk in conceptualization, planning, execution, and termination. For them "the PLC can be described in terms of the extent to which each phase differs in terms of the level of resources employed, the degree of definition, the level of conflict, the rate of expenditure, and so on". Let us examine each phase of PLC and the nature of risk associated with it; the strategy or proposed strategy that can be employed to manage risk to improve the probability of success by achieving the criteria defined for the success of a project.

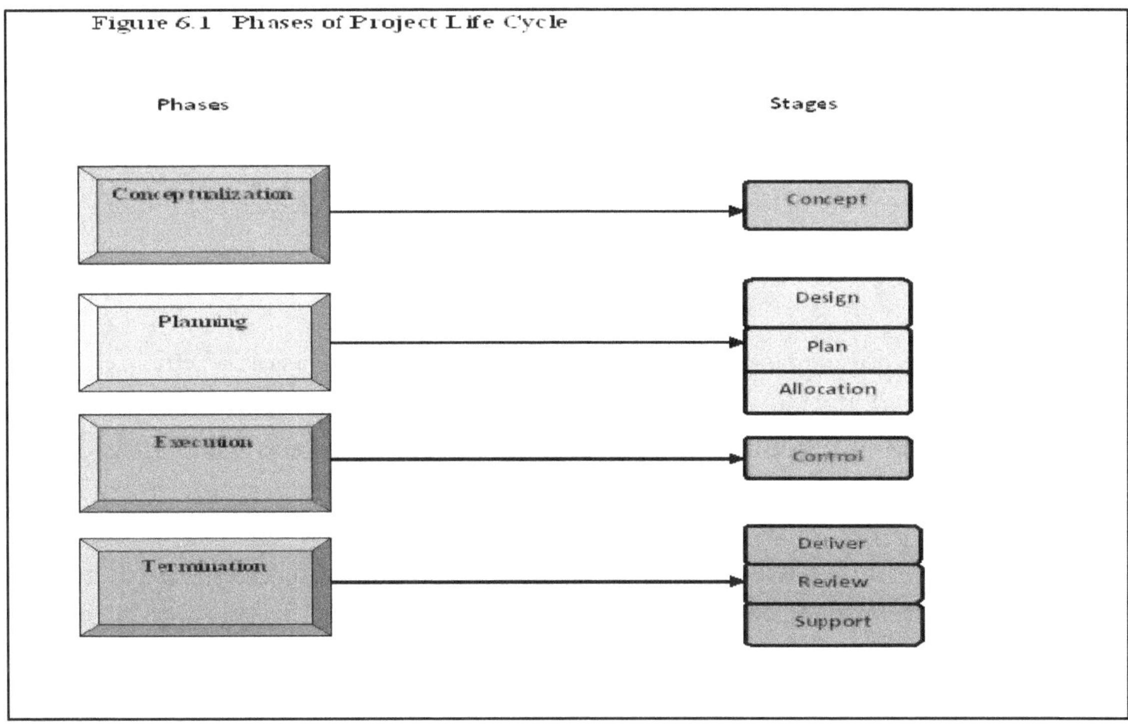

decomposed four phases into eight stages; for instance, the conceptualization phase includes concept stage, planning includes: design, plan and allocation, execution encompass control, and termination has: deliver, review and support (Figure 6.1).

Concept phase

According to Chapman and his colleague (1995) it "involves identifying a deliverable to be produced and the benefits to be expected from the deliverable". The deliverable may be a building, a website, software, 100 pieces of garments, 100kg of meat, 1500 meters of cloth, 25 miles of mettle road, an airport, a bridge, a qualification etc. The benefit of the project varies with the nature of the inheritance, the resources employed, the scope of impact, the timing of the project, the allocation involved, and the involvement of stakeholders or network partners i.e., customer, supplier, partner companies and the governmental bodies. Benefits may be financial, public centered, non-financial or as defined by stakeholders or agreed or agreed upon between project management and clients. The benefits may be immediate or long-term; the former is those which begin with the completion of the project. While long-term benefits start after recovery of the cost involved, such projects include dams, nuclear plants, and others. The process risk associated with this stage according to Ward and his colleague "moving on to a design before effective concept evaluation has taken place and the project concept and objectives have been crystallized".

Planning

When the concept stage seems workable, the team involved gives a green signal to 'go ahead' decision. It triggers the basic design that gives form to the proposed deliverable of the initiative. For instance, a performance criterion is developed to support the basic design. It tells the stakeholders the parameter of success related with the project. Most common performance criteria are listed to conceptualize the way progress will be measured. One way to demonstrate it is to determine the number of milestones over the life of the project. In the words of Ward and Chapman (1995) it "involves refining the project objectives, but it may involve the identification of additional objectives and further negotiation where pluralistic views persist". The project objective is to achieve by the project team, what will be mechanism to measure them and who will be responsible to do that. Another key job at this stage is to evaluate the entire design. The process risk involved "is that of moving on the plan stage before effective design evaluation has taken place. The decomposition of the planning phase into design, plan and allocation stages emphasizes this risk". (Ward and Chapman, 1995)

This stage shows the way design will be implemented. In other words, base plan is drawn with inclusion of targets and milestones that leads to development of plan. It also requires evaluation of a plan to justify its existence and finding out its negative aspects. For big projects more organizations can be involved such as dams and transport planes i.e., airbus. In small projects more people are involved to include more stakeholders. The risk involved "is moving on to the allocation stage before effective plan evaluation has taken place".

The allocation stage involves allocation of resources and contracts to various parties to move forward to achieving the plan. Besides basic allocation, a criterion is determined for it. Criteria may be based upon men-hours, number of square meters, the length of road, railway track etc. Three decisions are important at this stage: project organization, identification of participants and allocation of tasks. Allocation leads to execution risks between participants. "This activity is an important source or process risk, in that this allocation can significantly influence the behaviour of participants and hence impact on project performance". It determines the human involvement in the initiative, the most significant element in the success of a project. For instance, team formation and allocation of tasks to individuals and teams followed by resources they need for completion of their allocated tasks.

Execution

Ward and Chapman (1995) introduce the phase with they call it control stage. It implies that the project should be started now; efforts and expenditure increase in the control. The process risk exists in coordination and control because procedure may not be adequate for the purpose. The most significant risk factor is the "introduction of design changes". The demand adjustments in production plan, payments to affected parties or contractors: it increases cost, a major dent in the body of the project. Basic objective may be jeopardizing at this stage due to changes in cost and timeframe that emerge in the course of execution. Extra care is needed to avoid or minimize the impacts on the entire PLC.

Termination

It is composed of three aspects: delivery, review, and support. The delivery involves handover of the completed 'final deliverable' to the clients. Management demonstrates the actual performance of the delivered product. The actual performance may be according to original specification or something less or something more. The principal job of project manager is to verify what is being delivered. The deliverable may exceed the agreed upon functionalities or characteristics, an ideal achievement. The other side of the coin is dreadful if the product does not deliver its planned performance. The job of project manager and others is to explain the reasons for malfunctioning. And whether it can be improved soon. Nevertheless, the modification must be approved by stakeholders with a specific period.

The review involves a structured audit of the project after the completion of handover. The findings are known as learning from the project that may be a starting point in the next project or a source of improvement later, in the rest of the PLC. Documentation of the audit in line with performance criteria is helpful in later iterations in project management or changes to be made in the particular project.

The support stage is concerned with maintenance and fixation of liability for it; support criteria are defined to assign maintenance job to relevant personnel. A little or no risk is involved at this stage unless maintenance is outsourcing to fragile contractors.

The model is a detailed analysis of process risk at various phases and stages of PLC. It examines the inter-dependencies and reorganizes the significance of risk in a structured way. Outlines risk embedded or explicit within the stages and offers a mechanism to address it. However, understanding and application of the model is comer some. Development of link among various phases (stages) needs a lot of effort to grab reality of what are happening at each step and how to coordinate risk management ate these steps. Despite its shortcomings the model provides a way of risk, identification (which has been provided by authors), assessment and management. Thus, it can be used as a tool to manage projects with or without large investment in the area. The model may be more useful when used as a complementary instrument with other risk management strategies. For example, the framework offered by Frank (1987); he suggests Delphi method to assess risk for the planning, execution, and closure of projects. More people, other than the project team, can be involved to assess risk because 'two heads are better than one'. It can also be augmented with risk profiles or risk profiling at each phase or stage to define strategies for each of them. Such a model can be diagrammed as shown in Figure 6.2.

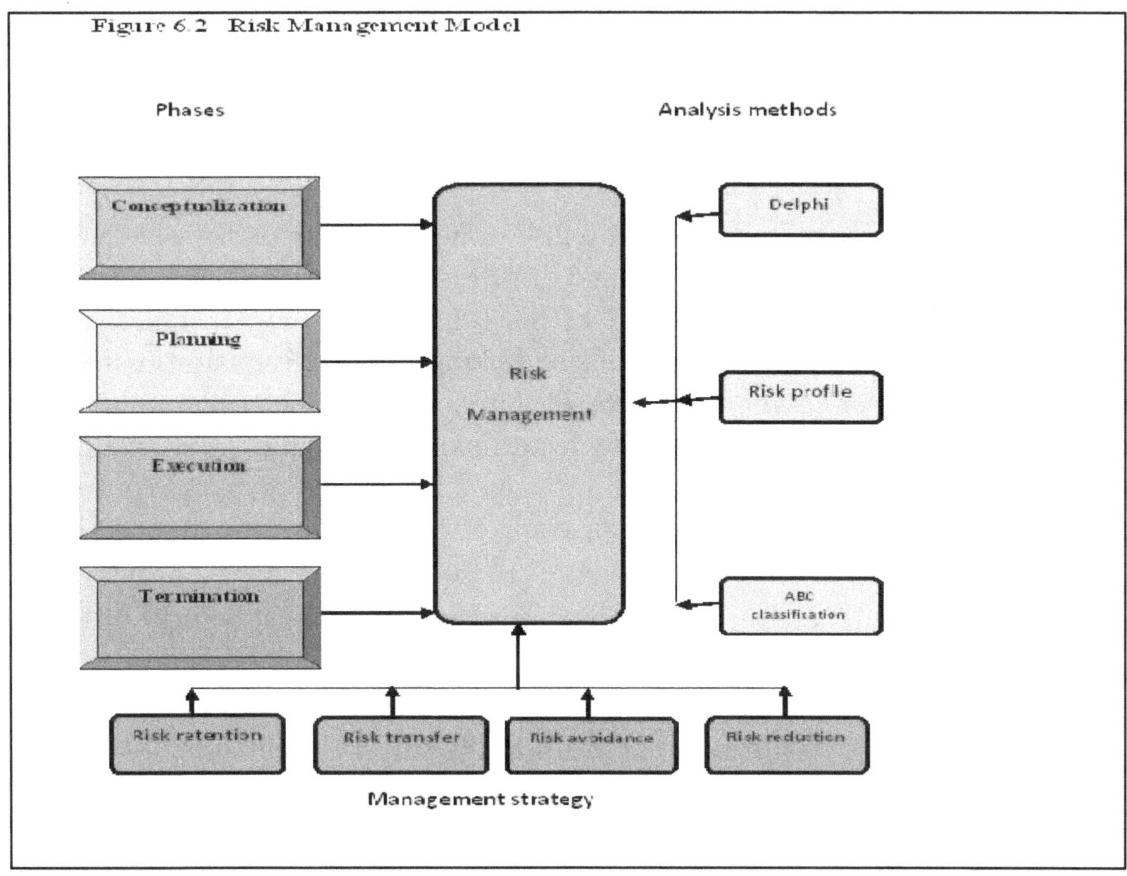

The model synthesizes the views of three writers to form a framework for an effective project risk management approach. We believe that managing risk based on the PLC is a workable idea since process risk exists within phases or stages. However, the risk found may not fulfill the scientific requirements because the method is subjective in nature. A more verifiable method is needed for identification and assessment of process risks to manage it scientifically. Delphi and other methods mentioned in the proposed model help to analyze and assess risk. It is followed by adoption of one or more options for managing risk. This may be useful for analysis, research, and application in the model in the practice to find out relationship among various elements and their effectiveness on the project performance or organization efficiency. The risk can be analyzed from qualitative and quantitative perspectives since both have their individual benefits. However, a collective outcome of both types of analysis provides useful input for making informed decisions.

Another important concept in project planning is the work down structure (WBS). It has been defined as "a work breaks down structure is a deliverable oriented grouping of project elements that organizes and defines the total scope of the project" (PMBOK, 2000).

In other words, it is selected with milestones and activities involved in each of the milestones. Deliverable is defined in ABL case study into ten milestones; each of the milestones delivers a part of the total project. For instance, milestone 'c' provides a definition of the website, testing shows demonstration of the website in real time situation. The WBS sets limits of the project; how many texts boxes, how many wages and how many hyperlinks. The product categories highlight the range of products on offer. WBS is used for both planning and control; planning parameters provide the basis for control. For instance, the planned budget for a given project is £800m; the figure is the standard against which cost control measures will be directed. In other words, the cost must be kept up to the above limit otherwise the project will overlap the cost. The job of the project manager is to keep an eye on cost through measuring and controlling measures. Responsibility charts and network diagrams including Critical Path Method (CPM) and Gantt Charts are stem from WBS. Therefore, it guides toward the right control mechanism to keep the project on track.

Risk in a project is concerned with the unexpected events that may occur due to known or unknown reasons, which create par time, or negative impacts on project plan (Ahmad El, 2007). Uncertainty may be acceptable, moderate, or unacceptable; the levels of ride are associated with outcomes i.e., Technical, schedule or cost (Nicholas, 2001). There is an alternative process of risk management as opposed to the one described above. The purpose of this is to make available alternative ways to address risk. Ahmad et al (2007) suggest the choice; it consists of five stages; establishing context, identifying risks, analyzing risk, evaluating risks and treating risks.

Establishment of context is concerned with representation of project units as well or their inter-relationships. It is useful for resource usage, requirement of equipment, availability of budget, involvement of stakeholder's knowledge of contract deferrable, strategic goals and schedule. They have suggested six techniques for establishment of context including project network diagrams, generalized activity networks and design structure mate races.

Risk identification involves determining possible deviation from the envisioned plans during the projects; it can be done with a checklist, influence diagrams, case-end-effect diagrams, failure mode and effect analysis, hazards operability study, fault trees and event tree.

It is followed by risk analysis, which is concerned with determining the risk factors on the entire system. Several techniques are available for this purpose: probability and impact grids, estimation of system reliability, fault tree analysis, event tree analysis, and sensitivity analysis and simulation.

Analysis is followed by risk evaluation i.e., prioritized risks events. Evaluation is possible with past experiences, lessons learned, best practices, organizational knowledge, industry benchmarks and standard practices. Several evaluation techniques have been developed overtime, decision tree analysis, portfolio management, and multiple criteria decision-making methods. Finally, risk mitigation process is applied to treat risks to minimize effects on the overall performance of the project concerned. Figures include the risk management treatment elements.

Review and discussion questions

1. Risk is the fourth constraint in managing projects. Discuss.

2. It is widely believed that risk lives in the phases of project life cycle. Describe key elements of each stage; which one is most important.

3. Project risk can be managed through an alternative channel i.e., Input-process- output mechanism. Choose a project of your choices and show risk in each of these stages i.e., Input risks, process risks and output risks.

4. Describe principal risk management techniques. Compare them briefly.

5. Reduction, avoidance, transfers, and retention is commonly considered managing risk. Which one is economically better off?

CHAPTER 7 SUMMARY AND LEARNING

A survey of accessible literature has been made in the previous pages to look into the pros and cons of the subject. Project management is an organized activity with starting and ending dates with one or more objectives to achieve. PMI views it as a temporary endeavor; it is temporary because it ends whenever it is completed. It is a project because it is injected in the organization to keep or improve its production and distribution power of products and services.

Project management evolved as a modern discipline in the early days of last century when Henry Gantt developed the well-known project planning and scheduling technique 'the Gantt Chart'.   The late nineteen fifties brought the technological revolution in telecommunications and physical movement of hardware; thus improved the scheduling technology. The CPM and PERT were also developed that enabled managers to plan and control big projects. WBS was introduced in the sixties in addition to the formation of PMI and IMPA. The eighties saw the production and publication of Project Management Body of Knowledge while the nineties were famous for project development methodologies such as PRINCE2. A cost management framework was added in the first decade of the new millennium in addition to improvements in PRINCE2. A project manager handles traditional business functions – planning, organizing, leading, and controlling – in addition to project related responsibilities. He focuses on projects with the usual tools and techniques. He has a range of qualities such as creating an inspired vision, is a good communicator, is an enthusiastic person and so on. Project manager can measure performance of individuals and team members with 'hard' or 'soft' tools.

Project initiation in the formal commencement of an endeavor; it starts from section. A project is usually selected by evaluating alternatives. The alternatives are evaluated with qualitative and quantitative approaches. Other key elements to be considered include alignment of the project with business strategy and preparation of project initiation documents. It is followed by project planning, a process of deciding in advance. What to do in the various stages of project life cycle. Project planning involves defining project objectives, project schedule, personnel required, evaluation process and methods and a risk management plan.

Project organizing revolves around assignment of tasks and activities, determining organization structure (full time or integration with existing work arrangement) and managing material resources. Activity schedules, PERT charts, and GANTT charts are available techniques to project managers. Resource allocation provides a smooth spreading of various resources over the life of a milestone on a periodic basis.

Project monitoring and control looks back to the planning parameters and progress. It begins with developing/preparing the right reports to know how things are going. They are matched with planned parameters: the discrepancies are corrected to put the project on the track. Project control techniques are helpful to take controlling measures. The control process can be reinforced if project success factors are seen or applied. It is augmented while keeping in mind the reasons of project failure elements.

The case study put together the key components of the discipline; it applies the project management tools, techniques, principles, and philosophies. It is organized around project planning, organizing, and controlling sections; the UK project management association has recommended this arrangement. The case study has been analyzed under the sub section of "discussion about the case study".

There are number of points appeared as learning from the case study.

1- Project management principles can be applied in small businesses or small projects.
2- Many small business managers do not know the available theories and the technological facilities for managing small projects.
3- Project management is a fascinating but progressive discipline where more research is needed for finding out the application of it in small businesses.

The learning points can be used in further research and practice in the ever-changing field but less understood in small businesses.

CASE STUDIES

1 CHEETHAM MEAT & POULTRY (CPM)

The nature of the case

The principles of PM are applicable in any organization irrespective of its size, nature of business or mode of organization (sole proprietor, partnership, public limited). It is the common view that project management is applicable in large projects, in bigger organizations. A few studies address the application of project management concepts in retail industry. This case study   examines it from a retail perspective. There are many industries that implicitly or explicitly apply project management principles; the authors have chosen meat retailers to examine the phenomenon. It is a mini case study on a mini entity.

Cheetham meat and poultry (CMP) was established in 2005 to serve the local community with a view to capture lion share of the market. Most of the other meat shops were not functioning as an independent concern, they work as a part of a cash and carry or a retail outlet. However, CMP deals with meat and poultry products only. CMP is in the heart of Cheetham village; it has a huge storage facility (cold store) where they can hang 40 lambs at a time. CMP has a 10 feet long display refrigerator and cutting worktop of the same size, five personnel are working in addition to the owner manager Mr. Shan. CMP owns an electronic cutting machine, a mince machine, a lot of knives and other cutlery. Two electronic cash registers are available for customer service. Beef, mutton, fish, and whole chicken are principal raw materials. The company manufactures 15 products including simple   mutton, beef, ribs, mince, and spare parts of animals. Chicken products include boneless thy, boneless chest, wings legs, whole chicken, baby chicken, spare parts such as hearts and stomach are the key chicken products.

Fish products are limited: whole fish, marinated fish and spiced fish are available. Although financial results are not available yet, the management was satisfied with the performance and perceives it to be a successful business.

The company has not expended much in the last five years, except hiring of two personnel to meet the increased demand; customer waiting time during peak hours is 15 to 20 minutes; the business customer usually receive their deliveries on time because they place their orders in advance.

The company received an order for 2000 kg of mixed products of mutton, chicken and fish. Table 1 shows the details of the project / order for analysis of the case study.

Table 1	**Details of the project**			
Item number	**Name**	**Quantity**	**Packing size**	**Delivery date**
1	Mutton	300kg	3kg	10.01.2011
2	Chaps	200kg	1kg	"
3	Mince	100kg	1kg	"
4	Chicken	500kg	1kg	"
5	Boneless meat	200kg	2kg	"
6	Drumstick	200kg (800 pieces)	2kg (10 pieces)	"

7	Fish spiced	50kg	2kg	"
8	Fish without spiced	50kg	2	"
9	Chicken mince	200kg	2kg	"
10	Chicken wings	200kg	2kg	"

Project planning at CMP

The purpose of planning, according to Anderson (1995) and his colleague are to gain ordinary understanding, obtaining overview of the work to be completed. It lays down the foundation for resource allocation and forming proper organization structure for the project that provides guidelines for subsequent work and defining a programme of monitoring and control.

The manager of CMP called a meeting to discuss the project and related issues. The meeting was attended by all the members of the staff since the project was to be completed with daily or normal tasks (the details will be discussed later under the project organization). The manager described the details of the project as mentioned in table 1. The project will have to be completed within four weeks in addition to the normal workload; the existing members of the team would carry it out without added hiring or overtime arrangements. The manager believes it is workable because all members of the staff are busy only at peak times, usually 1100 to 1600 daily. The shop opens at 0900 and closes in 1800 daily, seven days a week; it supplies a 4-hour slake time daily for each employee.

Mr. Shah, the manager estimates that CMP would need 30 lambs for mutton products, 1800 chickens and 100 whole fish to deliver the order. The project was managed by five personnel excluding the manager; it took 100 men hours; 1380 packets were made; each item was packed in durable plastic boxes and each packet was delivered to the customer.

CMP will have men 112 hours available within next four weeks, off which 80% of the time will be needed for the project.

The manager, Mr. Shah, informed the staff members about time available and the details of work. Mr. Jan said, "we need to make contingency plan for staff members to cope with uncertainties". Mr. Shah replied he had a plan to hire one or two personnel who will work with us as a fulltime member. In this case, we would have 40 more hours available weekly. We can double this by adding another person in our team; all members agreed with the contingency plan and were hopeful for the project to complete on time.

Although all members of the staff were trained to work on any product or able to cope with any raw material, four people were specialist for dealing with four types of raw material as shown in the table 2. The purpose of the table is to ensure that the "right staff" is available at the right place.

Table 2	Specialism of staff members	
Serial No	**Name**	**Animal type**
1	A. Khan	Cows
2	Mr. Bakka	Lambs
3	Arif Wala	Chicken
4	Akbar Sindhu	Fish

job of the meeting was to allocate the resources. The project uses a range of resources, the worktop, electronic cutting machine, cold store, packing material etc. some of them are shared and others can be used independently; the worktop is big enough to accommodate all personnel at a time. The cutlery is also enough to serve the entire team. However, electronic cutting machines can serve one person at a time. The team members can use it in turn whenever they need it. It saves time without significant loss of productivity. The finished products are stored in a cold store, which has a large capacity and is capable of storing 8000 kilograms of meat. All the personnel agree to complete the job along with the daily workload. CMP management offers 10% bonus to complete the project for everyone.

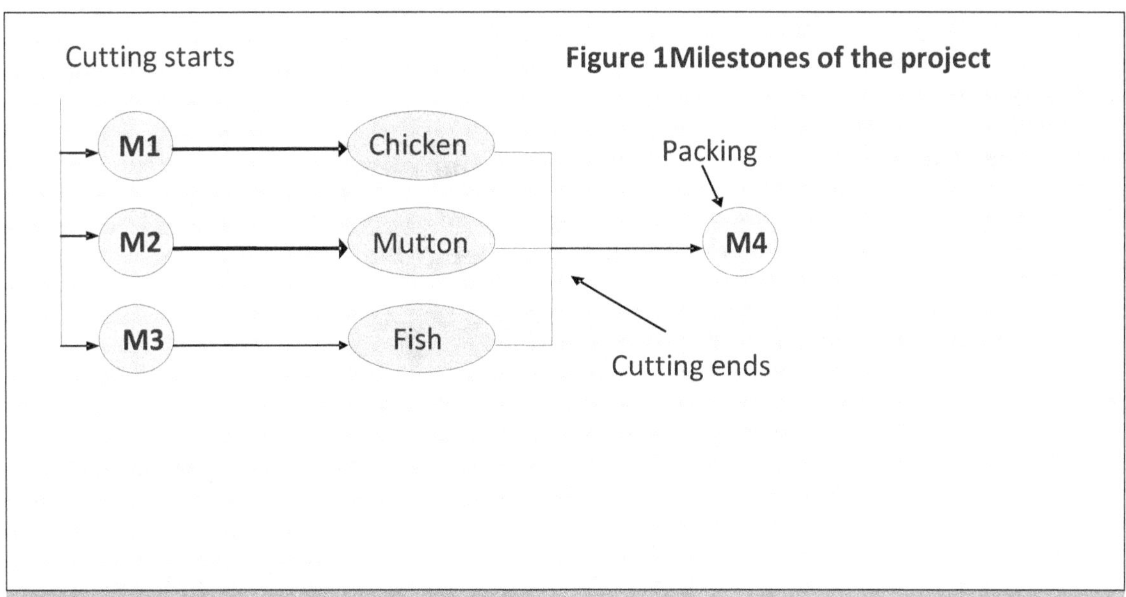

As can be seen from the above discussion two teams were formed; one is to cut or manufacture various products and the other to pack them. The first team virtually includes of all the personnel of organization headed by the manager where he did not do any physical work. The second team consists of four personnel in charge of CMP manager. The details about it will be discussed in the second section of this chapter.

Project activity and milestone planning

Milestones are the key achievements or stages of completion. Anderson (1995) and his colleagues view a milestone as "check point in the project, which enables us to ensure that we are on the right track. A milestone is a description of the state the project should be in at certain stages." Milestone should be defined in connection with the solution the project is offering.

Given that conceptual understanding, CMP defined milestone according to the packing plan described in figure 1 and 2. The largest quantity is chicken-based products followed by mutton and fish. Management has divided the cutting part of the project into three milestones: chicken, mutton, and fish, since the former represents 60% of the order followed by mutton 30% and fish 10%. The chicken will be started and finished first; the mutton will be in the middle and fish at the end.

Figure 2 depicts the milestones; the length of the bar is according to the percentage of time involved in a milestone. It is noted that there is only one dependency in the

125

milestones; packing needs completion of cutting M1-M3; they had to be completed at one point of time, the M4 can be started then. There is no dependency in the first three milestones, however.

Figure 2	Milestone bar chart			
	Period 1	**Period 2**	**Period 3**	**Period 4**
M1 Chicken	███	███	███	
M2 Mutton		███	███	███
M3 Fish			███	███
M4 Packing				███

Project organization

Organization refers to, in management literature, the distribution of responsibilities. In terms of project management the division of activities and tasks. Anderson and his colleagues (1995) believe a project is organized or responsibilities are allocated as full time or part time bases. Team members are relieved from all activities or normal jobs to work on a certain project as a full-time member. Alternatively, they can work on the project as a part-time in addition to their daily routine. It is termed the integration of a project to the existing operations.

CMP management decided to choose the second option because the company must serve daily customer as a mainstream function. If they chose full time choice than they must hire added staff for the project or some existing members have to be dedicated for the project. This would put added pressure on them, which jeopardizes the equality of work for which the CMP is famous. Secondly, the managers believe that the project is manageable with the existing workload and within the required time framework. Other members of the team were also agreed and happy with the arrangement as it does not disturb their daily routine.

The next question for the CMP manager was to choose mode of organization; theoretically, hierarchical and matrix methods are available. Matrix was selected because its merits outweigh its demerits; it is a better possibility for decision-making and fixes responsibilities, provides better communication, flexible organization and better use of resources (Anderson et al, 1995). It was important to draw a responsibilities chart to specify key responsibilities for various members of staff which were divided according to the milestones. Tables 3-6 show the responsibilities charts of various staff members individually and collectively.

Table 3 Responsibility chart according to milestones					
Milestone	Staff 1	Staff 2	Staff 3	Staff 4	Staff 5
M1	√	√	√	√	-
M2	-	√	√	√	-
M3	-	-	-	-	√

...

Table 4 Responsibilities chart for M 1					
Activity	**Staff 1**	**Staff 2**	**Staff 3**	**Staff 4**	**Staff 5**
Whole chicken	√	√	√	√	-

Boneless breast	-	√	√	-	-
Dram sticks	-	-	√	√	-
Mince	-	-	√	√	-
Chicken wings	√	√	-	-	-

...

Table 5   Responsibilities chart for M2

	Staff 1	Staff 2	Staff 3	Staff 4	Staff 5
Activity					
Mutton	√	-	-	-	-
Mince	√	√	-	-	-
Champs	-	-	-	√	-

...

Table 6   Responsibilities chart for M3

	Staff 1	Staff 2	Staff 3	Staff 4	Staff 5
Milestone					
Fish spiced	-	-	-	-	√

Fish simple	-	-	-	-	√

The last milestone is packing. Table 6.7 shows the responsibilities of the people involved.

Table 7	Responsibility chart of milestones			
Staff	Cow	Lams	Chicken	Fish
1	√			
2			√	√
3		√		
4				√

Project control

Although the project was a medium size venture, yet some controlling mechanism was essential to ensure the project was on track. The pros and cons of it was decided; each member of staff would fill in a progress chart daily showing the amount of work he has done on the project. This chart has to be checked by the manager daily and instructs the relevant members to catch up the work in case someone is behind the schedule.

Project control "involves analysis the situation, deciding what to do and doing it." It is management of project not merely paper works (Anderson et al, 1995). Control requires reporting of progress and taking correct measures, if necessary. A mechanism must be established to ensure timely reporting of progress at milestone level or periodically. Movement of milestone date, changing objectives, injecting additional resources and rearranging the workload of team members are typical controlling actions (ibid., p.152). Although controlling activities involve the use of resources, time management, schedule adherence, quality control, responsibility chart, changes/additions, waiting time and any special problems in large projects, yet CMP designed a daily progress report, which usually filled by the team members and examined by the manager to ensure progress at milestone levels. Table 8 reflects a progress report for the first day of the project.

Table 8 The progress report day one			
Team member	Total workload (kg)	Completed (kg)	Balance (kg)
Staff 1	450	50	400
Staff 2	450	100	350
Staff 3	450	50	400
Staff 4	450	50	400
Staff 5	200	20	180
Totals	2000	270	1730

The progress report for day 2 starts with the balance of the previous day and generates a new balance at the end of the day. The cutting work was completed in three weeks; the final week was reserved for packing. Eight hundred Kilograms were prepared in the second week and the balance was cut in the third week. The packing was done in the fourth week, while the delivery was due in the same week. The project was completed and delivered on time.

Discussion about the case study

The project was a medium size venture for the organization; however, most of the project management tools and techniques were applied. An important aspect of the project was its completion within time that was the major success criteria for it. Other parameters such as budget and quality were not especially important because the products of the project were to be used in the marriage function. The client needed it on time; quality was involved in cleaning the meat of fat and other unnecessary elements. All the personnel were supposed to do that for which they were well trained and experienced, so the quality was not an issue. Budget was also not incredibly significant element because the team members were paid as usual; however, a bonus was paid on the successful completion of the project. Since the project was completed on time, the staff was paid a bonus; the project did not overrun budget.

Milestones were identified and defined prudently based on the competencies of the staff; milestones were allocated to all staff members equally but not to the manager because he used to spend a lion share of time in managerial activities. Consequently, little time stays for operational duties; however, he has done it amicably.

The resources were used effectively; the time of each staff member was applied to the best of their capabilities; thus, the project flew in the planned direction over its life cycle. Tables 9 and 10 show the analysis of the project from various perspectives.

Table 9	Product wise analysis of project

Items	chicken	Mince	Boneless breast	Drumsticks	Wings	Simple mutton	Champs	Spiced fish	Simple fish	Total

Chicken	500kg	200kg	200kg	200(800 pieces)	100					1200
Mutton		100				300	200			600
Fish								100	100	200

...

Table 10	Allocation of workload				
Items	**Staff 1**	**Staff 2**	**Staff 3**	**Staff 4**	**Staff 5**
Chicken	300	300	300	300	
Mutton	150	150	150	150	
Fish					200
Total workload	**450**	**450**	**450**	**450**	**200**

Note:

A. The duration of the project was 4 weeks

B. Each staff member has to cut 450kg extra meet except staff 5.

The duration of each activity is based upon the assumption that a member of the staff can cut 25kg of any meat on average. Given that table 11 shows the total men hours required and total men hours available for the project. Also, table 12 shows the assumptions of various calculations.

Table 11	Activities and their duration	
Activity no	**Activity name**	**Activity duration**
1	Whole chicken	20 men hours

2	Chicken mince	8 men hours
3	Boneless breast	8 men hours
4	Drumsticks	8 men hours
5	Wings	4 men hours
6	Mutton mince	4 men hours
7	Simple mutton	12 men hours
8	Champs	8 men hours
9	Fish simple	4 men hours
10	Fish spiced	4 men hours
11	packing	4 men hours
Total		84 men hours

...

Table 12	**Assumptions of men-hours calculation**
	1. A staff member can cut 25 kg of any animal in one hour.
	2. Total weight of the project 2000kg
	3. Men hours required for cutting the project=2000/25=80.

4. Men hours needed for packing 20.

5. Total men hours required for the project=100.

6. Available men hours during the life of the project=5 (persons) x 8(daily working hours) x 20(number of working days within which the project is to be completed) =160 men hours i.e., 5x8x20 =800 men hours.

7. Extra time available for daily work=160-100=700 men hours

The above analysis suggests that CMP did more work by applying the principles of project management because daily work was not disturbed, and the project was completed as more work.

Review (case) questions

1. Do you think project management principals have been appropriately applied to CMP?

2. What other PM principals could be applied to the case study? Provide an example.

3. Has the project management process including planning, organizing, and controlling been implemented adequately? If not, what alternatives were available and could be applied for the efficient use of project resources.

4. The management of CMP opted "integration" strategy. Do you agree with the decision? Why and why not?

2 Project Management in Abacus Browsers Limited (ABL)

ABL was established in early nineties to offer Software Development Company as a limited company. In 1996 with the advent of the internet the operation was expanded to web development, web hosting and maintenance, training to clients and organizations. The number of staff was doubled to 25 personnel; system analysts, programmes, web developers, graphic designers, taxing, and business development officers are the key players. The annual sales exceeded 6-million-pound last year; 40% of sales comes from web development services which is mercers 10% annually, the only area that did not affect due to recent secession.

ABL develops small and medium size websites and offers hosting for the same market. The customers come from a variety of industries including manufacturing, trade and services, the average life of a project is 8 weeks with a standard deviation of 2 weeks that involves about 8-10 personnel. The acquisition team which is also known as business development team responsible for contract winning the specification is agreed/decided with the help of a developer; the organization has been divided into five teams: web development, programming, texting, maintenance, and hosting. All teams are reporting to the chairman, the head of the organization (Table 1).

<table>
<tr><td colspan="2">Table 1 Specification of the proposed website</td></tr>
<tr><td>1.</td><td>Overview</td></tr>
<tr><td>2.</td><td>Optimization - accessible, budget of link building</td></tr>
<tr><td>3.</td><td>Number of web pages: home page, product list, product details pages, online shop, about us, contact us, site map,</td></tr>
<tr><td>4.</td><td>Style and layout</td></tr>
<tr><td colspan="2">Overall style</td></tr>
<tr><td colspan="2">Navigation-links to home page, product list, about us, contact us</td></tr>
<tr><td>5.</td><td>Additional characteristics</td></tr>
<tr><td colspan="2">Accessibility- W3C standards</td></tr>
<tr><td colspan="2">Valid code - available to w3c specification</td></tr>
</table>

The overview must show the purpose of the site; as a sample it should say "we want people to find out our products by searching the web. The site will provide detailed information about the products and enable visitors to make an on live purchase" (Vordweb, 2010).

ABL received an order of a medium size website to be delivered within four weeks of a trading organization. The customer has provided the list of requirements as shown in table 2.

<table>
<tr><td colspan="2">Table 2 Requirements of the project</td></tr>
<tr><td>1.</td><td>History of the company</td></tr>
<tr><td>2.</td><td>List of major customers served in the past and some of them are being served</td></tr>
</table>

3.	The list of major products the company sales
4.	A list of the staff in service
5.	How the customer can be accessed
6.	Organization structure of the company
7.	Major links to useful organization
8.	Order tracking system
9.	Three D display of each product with details of its features
10.	Payment and financial issues
11.	Order or shopping procedures
12.	Goods selecting process
13.	Customer services
14.	FAQ

It is the business practice within ABC that a general meeting of all heads of the teams is held upon receipt of a new project which can be called a project initiation meeting. Each project is given a name by the business development team to distinguish it from other project. This project has been called as SHARP for this purpose.

The usual meeting was held to discuss SHARP on Monday morning at 10:00. Mr. Farkat, the head of the ABL inaugurated the meeting and introduced the project to the participants, the meeting has held to decide various phases of the project such as conceptualization, planning, execution and termination. In addition, risk identification and management is the part of the agenda. An analysis of the project was undertaken to decompose it into more professional teams. Mr. Kakor, the head of system analysis team identify the details of the project. He proposed a tentative list of the website components as shown in table 3.

Mr. Faraket suggests formation of a team to oversee the project; the other member agreed with him. A team called SHARP was formed whose members were heads of various team.

It was also decided that the responsibilities will be assigned on the basis of teams rather than individuals; the usual head of the tam will be the coordinator of that particular team. The meeting was adjourned until next day when project will be planned.

Table 3 The components of the website		
Item	Components	Items %
1. The title	1	0.3
2. Number of banners	20	7
3. Number of text boxes	15	5
4. Number of marquees	2	0.7
5. Number of slide shows	2	0.7
6. Logan of strategic partners and links	7	2
7. Product categories	4	1.4
8. Hyper links	180	61
9. Frames	3	1
10. Images	50	17
11. Colors	10	3.4
Total items	**294**	**100**

The next meeting was held where it was decided that the project will be implemented according to project life cycle approach. PLC according to pm1 consists of four phases: concept, planning execution and termination. There are taken in turn in the following pages.

Project Initiation

Initiation is concerned with identification of deliverable and the benefits associated with the project (Ward and Chapman, 1995); or according to PMI (2010) inputs (product description, strategic plan, project selection criteria, historical information) and output (project charter, assignment of a project manager, constraints and assumptions). The owners of SHARP decide inputs who would have described the project and apply the selection criteria to obtain the economic justification of the project. ABL has to describe the project in order to give it a separate identity; the description of the project in non-technical terms may be as follows.

> The project is a website that provides identity to the organization on the web and an instrument for e-commerce and e-business.

The details of the project have been provided in table 2 as provided by the customers concerned. Benefit of the project to ABL is that it would contribute towards the annual revenue and strengthened image of the organization as a leading provider of web services.

Since the organization is a small company and projects it works is also always small or at the most medium size, therefore, imitation of a new project is briefly dealt. Detailed   analysis is not made which is usually done in project initiation document (PID) table 3 has been prepared to describe the project.

Project planning at ABL

The objective of planning is to understand the project, the details of the work to be accomplished and the time scale. If provides the basis recourse allocation and commitment of different teams. The work is divided into milestones and teams are establishes, monitoring and control mechanism is defined (Andersen et al, 1995). It may include detailed design, a workable plan and allocation of resources (Ward and Chapman). PM1 provides a more elaboratcd view of the planning process: scope, activity details, budget issues, project risk, schedule development etc. However, all the components are not applicable to ABL; they are considered in the following paragraphs.

The project team prepared a schedule of milestone and related details. ABL initiate a project when a customer approached for a new job or and his proposal in accepted which as always considered the first milestone. The second is to define the project in technical or professional terms for various teams to understand the requirements. A meeting is usually called to look into the customers' requirements and translate them into specification. Requirement are recorded in table 2 and the have been translated into specification in table 3. The third is to allocate parts of the project to various teams and allocate required resources, if they need additional hardware, software, or another requirement. Since almost identical project are done in ABL. A template has been developed for this purpose (See Table 4).

Table 4 Millstone template		
Deliverable millstone	**Completion date**	**Who is to do**
Predevelopment: a-Order b-Definition c-Team formation	Week 1 Week 1 Week 1	
Development: a-Design b-Development c-Programming d-Testing Execution: a-Delivery b-Implementation to clients	Week 2 Week 2 Week 2 Week 3 Week 3 Week 4	
c-System termination	Week 4	

A diagrammatic depiction of the milestone has been shown in Figure 1 when a new project is received in the business development section (team), the team is responsible for negotiation of project price, time scale and delivery mechanism. The team also collects or captures project requirements. Sometimes the customer may not know the characteristics of the website because it is a small organization where these is no IT department or even in some cases any advanced IT literate person. ABL team informs the clients that such and such capabilities can be included in the proposed website. In any case, implementable requirements are collected and to some extent negotiated with the customers. The price of the product is received in full or as agreed between the customer and ABL team.

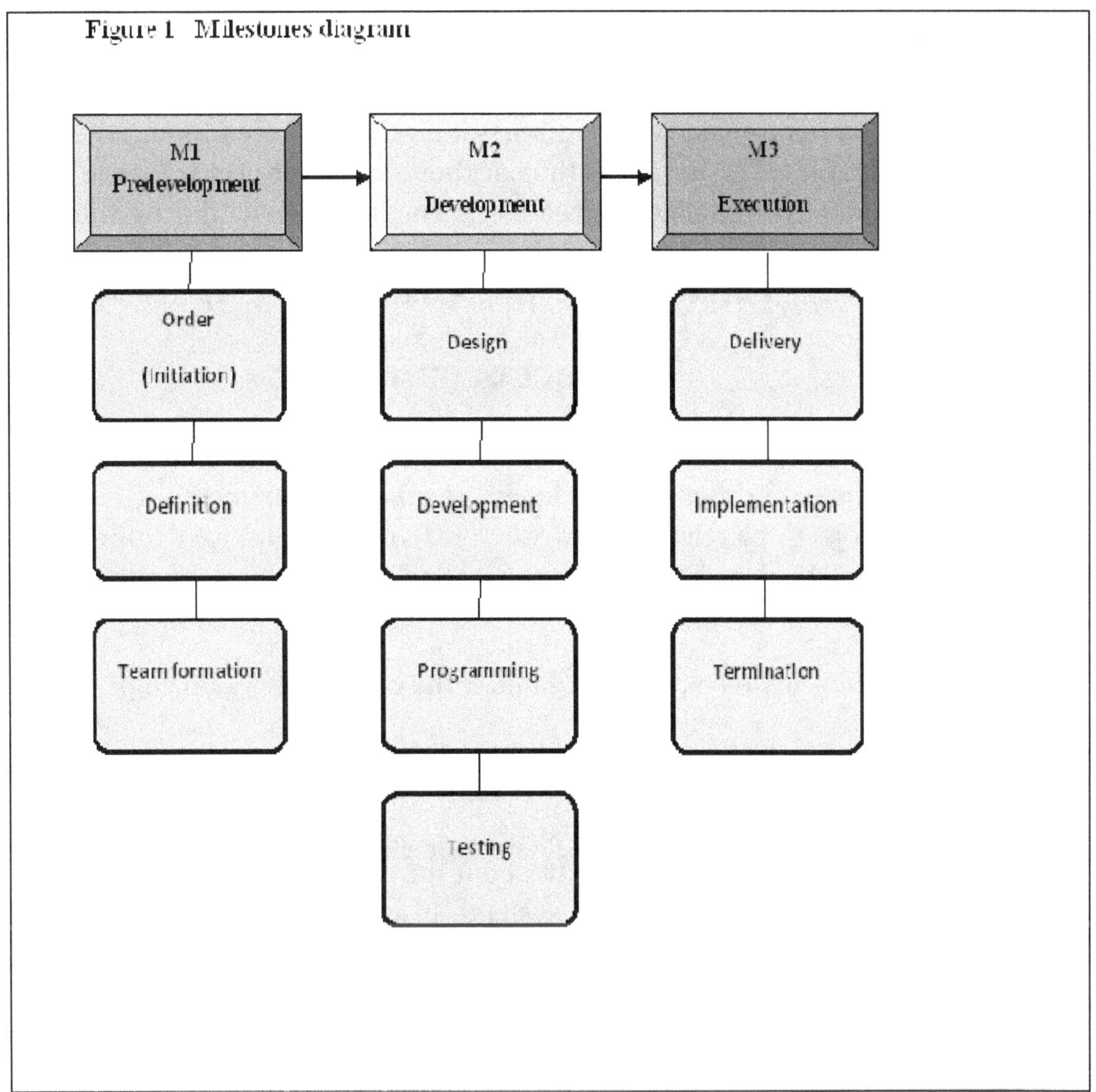

The same team defines the project in technical terms principally for development team, but it is exchanged with customers for approval. Mostly the ABL definition stays as it is; modification is needed rarely in very few cases. Anyway, any changes or suggested modification are incorporated in the definition (Merchant, 1985). Thus, the project is defined officially. It is followed by formation of the project team (the details will be discussed later). Thus, the project is handed over to the project development team (PDM) which is known as the name of the project, so the SHARP team is responsible of the endeavors. Up to this state the project is known at predevelopment phase.

The development phase will be discussed in the next section and the final phase in the execution. The former is the backbone of the project life cycle because the actual product or tangible deliverable is "manufactured" during the phase. The later deals with client: delivery to the client, implementation of the website on the systems of client and debugging of the website, if it does require.

Project organizing

Organizing refers to the decisions making to determine the arrangement of responsibilities to different individuals, teams or departments. The purpose is to achieve project objective, which resources will be employed to do that. It also includes mechanism for management and coordination of activities (Smith, 2007).

Five key tasks are to be performed under the banner of organizing:

1. Determination of assignments or responsibilities
2. Deployment and estimation of resources
3. Management of all of the above
4. Decision of senior management about the coordination of the project

ABL has a double tier system of arrangement of responsibilities: predevelopment phase and development phase. Business development team is responsible for predevelopment phase, while development is jointly done by other teams. The customers face team is responsible for delivery and post-delivery phase. It applies the organization structure for the project consists of three teams as shown in figure 2.

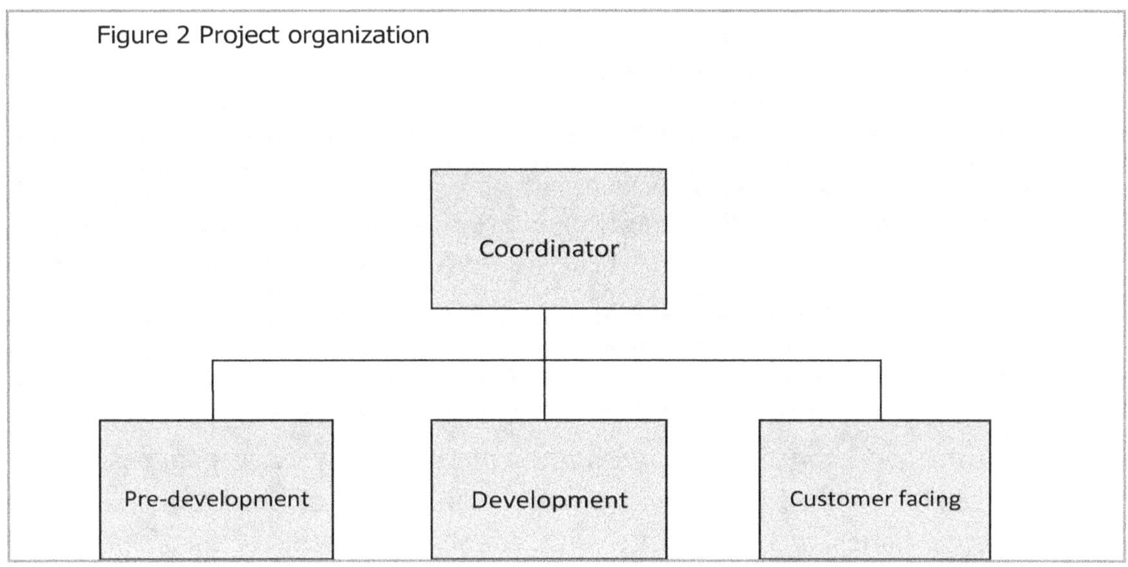

Each team picks up required people from the organizational teams i.e., designers, graphic or programming. Predevelopment team normally takes a week to negotiate with customer define the project in technical terms for development team and forms a team appropriate with the nature and size of the project concerned. For instance, if the project needs intensive programming skills, then two members from the programming team are included in the development work. If above average graphics are required, a graphics intensive team is picked up and so on.

The development team is responsible to design, develop, programme and test the website. There are technical jobs, so IT professionals dominate the team; the coordinator of the project checks the progress on weekly basis. Individual members of the team remain in touch with each other on daily basis and the developments in the project are discussed as and when they need assistance from one another.

The execution team received the software as a finished product from the development team, however, executors' double check the functionality and ensures quality parameters. The website is delivered to the customers with help documents and FAQs. A member of the team helps the clients to implement the website; any abnormality is noticed and debugged. When everything works ok, the termination documents are exchanged say the software has been received by the client and is working as agreed initially.

The coordinator oversees all team, nevertheless, the project moves sequentially, he has to concentrate on one team at a time. Some parallel work is done in development phase when developer, programmers and designers work together. Any changes in design lead to corresponding changes in product characteristics or programmes codes.

Delivery of the product, however, widens the jurisdiction of coordinator to outside the four walls of ABL to customers. He ensures the delivery of the project on time and keeps in touch with implementers. Any discrepancy is resolved with the help of business development team who had initially negotiated the characteristics of the website with client as well as technical personnel from various teams from where the project went through. Thus, a project seems to a collected effort of the entire organization rather than masterpiece of a single person or a team.

Theoretically, the project sponsor or coordinator meet two alternatives to organize a project: hierarchical and matrix organisation. The later carries a range of benefits: improved communication, flexible organization. Better use of resources, improved decision making, and fixing responsibility is easy for managers (Anderson et al., 1995) given that the table 5 shows the teaming arrangement of SHARP, a matrix structure.

Table 1 Organization of SHARP						
Organization teams						
Project teams	Bus. Dev.	Design	Graphics	Systems Analyst	Testing	Programming

Predevelopment	X					
Development		X	X	X	X	X
Execution	X				X	

The predevelopment has been assigned to business development team; its functions have been described in the previous paragraphs. All other teams are involved in the development work. However, testing and business development take part in execution due to its nature.

A related issue in project management is preparing a responsibility chart according to milestones. The project has been divided into ten milestones which are listed in table 4. The next question is to assign each milestone one or more teams to do the job; the Table 6 through light on them.

Table 6 Responsibility chart of various milestones

Teams	Contract	Definition	Team formation	Design	Development	Programming	Testing	I	II	III
1. Business development	√	√	√							
2. Design				√						
3. S.A.				√						
4. Graphics					√					
5. Programming						√				
6. Testing							√	√	√	√

I= Delivery, II= Implementation, III= Termination

The table is self-explanatory and is an elaborated form of figure 3 above. The purpose of the responsibility chart is to pinpoint the job to be done; the assignment has been made according to teams rather than individuals because ABL is a small organization where teams are material than individuals.

Activity chart can augment the above arrangement at greater details. Table 3 shows the components of the proposed website; if we assume each part as an activity than a table can be prepared for them as has been a practice in ABL. Since the website components are selected with development phase, therefore, activity chart of the phase has been included here (see Table 7).

Table 7 Activity chart for design			
	Personnel		
Activities	Staff 1	Staff 2	Staff 3
Banners	√		
Text boxes		√	
Slide shows			√
Marquess			√
Frames	√		
Images		√	
Hyper links	√	√	√
Partners logo			√
Product list		√	
Colours	√	√	√
Title bar	√		
Mics	√	√	√

The workload is divided according to the available time of each person since all personnel work on several projects at the same time. ABL integrates new projects with the existing projects rather than arrangement of a project to a specific individual or team on full time basis. (See Tables 8 and 9).

Table 8 Millstone and their details			
Stage	**Deliverable (milestone)**	**Completion date/time**	**Responsibility**
PRE-DEVELOPMENT	a-Contract approval	Week 1	Business development team
	b-Project definition	Week 1	Business development team
	c-Team formation	Week 1	Business development team
DEVELOPMENT	d-Design	Week 2	Design team
	e-Development	Week 2	Graphics team
	f-Programming	Week 2/3	SA team
	g-Testing	Week 3	Testing team
EXECUTION	h-Delivery	Week 4	Business development team
	i-Implementation	Week 4	Testing team
	J-Termination	Week 4	Business development/testing team

...

Table 9 Phase bar chart				
Stage	Week 1	Week 2	Week 3	Week 4
PRE-DEVELOPMENT				
DEVELOPMENT				
EXECUTION				

Execution (control)

The first step in execution is to start work as per schedule and check whether everything is going as planned. According to Smith (2007) who refers Merchant (1985) in this connection control is "the systematic process through which managers regulate organizational (or project) activities to make them consistent with expectations established in plans and to help them achieve all predetermined standards of performance". Key function to know progress and they take corrective action, if necessary, movement of milestone date, changing objectives, injecting additional resources and rearranging of workload of teams or team member are the possible action that may be taken (Andersen et al., 1995). Ward and Chapman (1995) write that change in design of the project is the key source of project risk. Thus, managing it is important at this stage. ABL executed the project gradually as a part of the day-to-day business. The progress was checked on weekly basis; a progress report was designed for the purpose. For example, the design team reported the progress of the first week; the progress has been shown in Table 10.

Table 30 Progress report of week 1 of design team

Personnel	Activities							
	Banners		Text boxes		Marquees		Frames	
	Complete	Balance	Complete	Balance	Complete	Balance	Complete	Balance

Staff 1	10	10					3	X
Staff 2			8	7				
Staff 3					2	X		

Staffs 1 is responsible for banners and frames. He has completed half of the banners and all the frames at the end of the first week of project development (note that it is the second week of the project). It means the remaining work is to be completed in the second week of the development (in the third week of the project). Similarly, the staff 2 is responsible for text boxes; he has completed almost half of them, and the balance will be completed in the forthcoming week.

There are 294 total items in the project (See table 3), the total progress has been shown in tables 11 and 12.

Table 11 The balance of work at the end of the first week (the second week of the project)			
Activities	**Balance**		**Complete**
Banners	10	50%	10
Text boxes	7	47%	8
Hyper links	80	44%	100
Images	20	40%	30
Logos of strategic partners and their links	3	43%	4
Total balance (No. of	120	41%	152

items)			

...

Table 12The amount of work completed		
Activities	No. of item	Status
The title bar	1	√
Marquees	2	√
Slide shows	2	√
Product categories	4	√
Frames	3	√
Colours	10	√
Total	**22**	

The total number of items completed was 174; thus 59% of the work has been completed and 41% is still being for the second week (the third week of the project. The remaining work is shown in Figure 3)

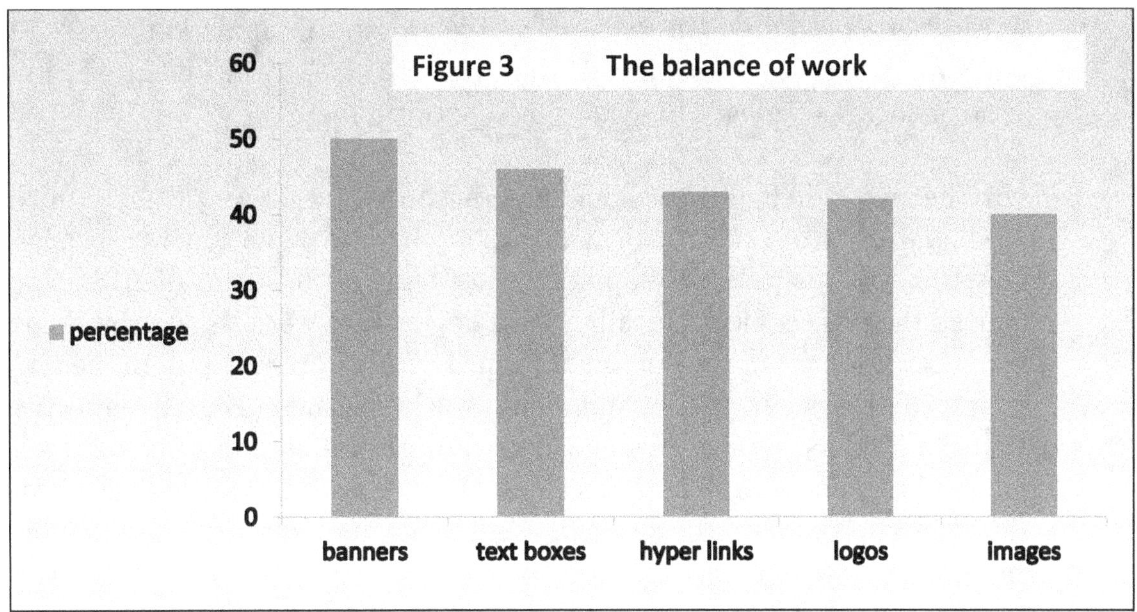

These diagrams are used to control the activities of the project and to check the progress. There was no discrepancy in any of the teams or individual; the reports were also sent to management to keep them informed about the status of this project as a part of the feedback procedures laid down in the project charter.

It is important to analyze the project at the outset for better implementation. For instance, Table 3 shows the percentage break down of the workload. The analysis is all about development phase for the purpose of this document.

The project was completed in the following week without any impediment and moved to testing team. The test drive was completed as per requirements of the client. The project met its quality standard as outlined by software charted bodies. Since it was ready to be delivered on time, therefore, the manufacturing cost did not increase and so the budget was in control. The project moved to the final phase, the termination.

Project termination

Ward and Chapman (1995) believe the phase involves three stages: delivery, service and support. Delivering of a project includes commissioning and hand over to clients. The product is showed to the customers where a step-by-step verification is required. In the words of Ward and Chapman (1995) it "involves verifying what the product of the project will do in practice: its actual performance, as opposed to its designed performance."

ABL the project in two steps; a half an hour presentation was given to the director of IT and his team of client organization. The presentation was prepared and presented by business development team and testing team of ABL. They have showed the project electronically where key feature were shown. A session of ten minutes was a part of the demonstration. The software was put on the air, loaded on the client system, and functionality was performed. The IT team was happy with the product, its features and design, the combination of colours and other components. The second half was to load the website, its various files through the administration box on the same day. All has to be done on Sunday morning so that the new site must be in place by early morning on the following day, the first day of the week. It was done successfully with the help of some personnel of the clients.

The service stage involves a thorough audit of the product, it is documented to know what the achievements, technical and others so that mistake can be avoided, and good learning is added to the experience of the individuals and teams worked on the project. The emphasis is on the lessons which are not obvious, so the meanings are identified between the times. ABL conducted such audit offer three days of implementation of the project because it was assumed that the time was enough to judge the performance of the site and to identify any complicacy in the functionality.

The support stage is concerned with maintenance and liability in the post delivery and service stages. Website maintenance involves uploading information which is time sensitive such as events, circulars, and news. It is usually the job of client's web master; however, it may need help of the developer if major changes are to be introduced or hosting is changed. Some developers such as ABL offer periodic maintenance of its client's websites virtually free of charge; the purpose of the strategy is to keep a connection with the customers. And it is a competitive advantage for the organization.

The case study assumes that ABL operates an eight-hour shift from Monday to Friday and employees can be hired in weekends on over-time basis for which they are paid special rates. The employee agreement has a clause in black and white.

Risk management at ABL

Risk is associated with the uncertainties in the variables of project or parameters of a given venture. Perry (1986) believes project risk may appear from "failure to keep within the cost estimates, failure to achieve the required completion date, failure to achieve the functional performance." He, however, suggests that individual project managers should develop the list of risks appropriate with their projects. Given that the risk in ABL are little bit different from the above but they are the added risks or sources of risk since ABL projects are also tend to the basic risks as mentioned above: cost, time and quality.

Risk may appear from at least three areas: cancellation of contract, learning of key personnel during a certain project and synchronization of a website with the system of clients. Since ABL's business is all about contracted jobs i.e., every website is developed as a special job or product. The customer has the right to cancel the job up to certain point, for instance during phase1, the pre-development. There are cancellation charges which are covering the risk element. The company loss is psychological, for example, the client might have cancelled the contract due to availability of cheap substitute or the company may have suggested liquidation or bankruptcy. These types of cases are about 2%. ABL has insured such cancellations, thus the monetary loss is recovered from the policy. The psychological loss is however, kept since there is little rescue available to manage it. The monthly or quarterly progress reports highlight the reasons for such cancellations with the explanation that there was no monetary loss due to these factors. Business development team tries to sign only those projects which are more certain. But human judgment may not be as correct as a mechanical solution, which, unfortunately does not exist in this particular situation.

The second source of risk is associated with changes in specification or changes in the availability of personnel. Changes in specification are dealt with more charges or increase in the cost to customer. If also affect the personnel working on the project because they must change features of the website and change are to be made in workload and planned activities.

A serious risk arises when key personnel such as the coordinator of a project leaves the organization or fall sick. The issue has been addressed by making sure that personnel should not leave ABL suddenly, must five at least four weeks' notice to make necessary changes in the workload of other employees. The second strategy to address the risk is the integration of new projects into the existing business operations rather than assigning the project to a single team. It jeopardizes the project under consideration and in fact the image of ABL.

Integration is more practical as Andersen et al. (1995) argue; under this arrangement new projects are added in the workload as a part time ventures. It also reduces the negative impacts of leaving any personnel in the development of a project.

The third category of risk rises in the implementation stage when the new site may not be integrated with the client's IT systems. It may be in the areas of software compatibility or excessive security mechanism in the client systems. The "entry barriers" are removed with the help of client organization. It is followed by audit or service to ensure things are going in order and to identify learning points for future reference and improvement in the process of project lift cycle. The learning is both technical as well as business oriented. The former is later applied in technical issues in the sub segment projects and the later are used for negotiation with potential customer. In this way ABL is a learning organization, a character of the agile project management. Agile projects are least tended to failure as reported by Amber (2008). Table 13 summarizes the risk management strategy of ABL with details of the resources of risk, the way of managing it and the risk management options applicable to each of them.

Table 5 Project risk management strategy in ABL		
Source of risk	**Managing risk (who bears the risk)**	**Risk management option**

Contract	Customers	Risk transfer
	Third party	Risk transfer
Changes in specifications	Customers	Risk reduction
Changes in personnel	ABL	Risk retention
Implementation	ABL/Customers	Risk reduction

Case questions

1. Do you think the risk management strategy of the ABL is appropriate if not why?

2. ABL had adopted phase approach for managing risk i.e., risk in conception or imitation, planning, organizing and control. Describe key features of each of these phases.

3. The software project was divided into milestones and activities. DO you think the milestones are suitable for the nature of the project?

4. What are the weaknesses in the management of the project? How can they be overcome?

5. Describe the strengths of the approach management has used to complete the project.

3 PROJECT MANAGEMENT IN SOFTWARE DEVELOPMENT EAGLES (SDE)

Software development Eagles (SDE) was setup by three friends studying in the Asian University of Hong Kong in 1995 after graduating.

None of the friends had enough money to invest in the business but they were motivated to some entrepreneurial venture rather than work for the others. They have completed three projects together in the university: system development software engineering and IT project management. Their projects were rated above average by their professors. One of them suggested them to start a software development business after graduation.

SME bank and department of industries, the government of Hong Kong was offering financial support for young entrepreneurs. The three friends who were known as eagles in the university borrowed 2 million from the bank and attended a series of seminars and workshops organized by the department of industries about the formulation and management of new companies. The friends also did work experience in the software house, which was partly managed by one of their visiting professors in the city. It was the time when Chinese were proposed themselves to take over the control of the Island from Briton after couple of years, in 1997.

The friends or eagles assume that there would be room for new entrepreneurs when the government would change hands because many existing businesses will move to London in addition to the ever-expanding Asian markets. Eagles won a contract of development of large website only after two months of incorporation of SDE. Since the project was a large endeavor and had to be completed in 12 weeks times, the eagles (as the company was famous after incorporation) hired two more system analysts, one of them brought ten years' experience and another have five years' experience in the development field. The names of friends were Lee, Long and Lau. Lee was selected as CEO; Mr. Long took over the responsibility of company secretary and Lau as technical director. This was done for the arrangement of the organization or to fulfill the legal requirement, but all the members work as normal on all the projects.

The client firm was called speed property LTD. (SPL); Mr. Lee compiled the requirements of the job (or project for the purpose of this writing) has prepared table to demonstrate and summarized them.

New projects are usually discussed in weekly meetings where progress of existing projects is examined and new are started. A meeting was scheduled on Monday March 21, 2011, in order to discuss the project; the agenda of the meeting consists of: planning the project, selecting the teams and project sponsors, allocating initial resources, reviewing existing control mechanism for this project and deciding the time frame.

Table 1 The Requirement of SPL project

S. No.	Name of Component	Number
1	Index page	1
2	Banners	45
3	Slides	2
4	Marquees	2
5	Frames	13
6	Search (Query box)	1
7	Products	6
8	Services	2
9	Text box	292
10	Hyperlinks	30
11	Colors	2

One of the founders used to be the sponsor of any new project, therefore, Mr. Long, the company secretary was s proposed the sponsor for this project, even though two of the recent addition to the workforce was more experienced. It was his first major project since the company was formed. He was selected because Lee and Lau had lots of projects to manage, and partners believe that "employees" cannot be trusted to assign such kind of responsibility. Long, has been active partner in the projects, which they have completed in the university. However, he was chosen secretary of the company because he was efficient negotiator (probably he was a better negotiator among three friends). A team of four other developers was assigned to him. The team was asked to identify the number of resources, she needs and their timings so that arrangements can be made for them. The meeting can be made for them. The meeting of friends was concluded after making these important decisions.

Mr. Long called a meeting of his team after four days to examine the project and start it formally. Other members of the team were trained in different areas of the website development; Mr. Jones was graphic designer, Mr. Yong was HTML writer, Mr. Shan was business analyst and Mr. Fast was database expert.

The Eagles have the tradition to implement projects according to life cycle approach i.e., ., project analysis and planning, project organizing, implementation, control and evolution. The last part was used for planning projects in the future because learning curve travels up with the completion of every project. Mr. Long setup a team of two individuals for analysis and planning of the endeavor.

The mini team believed that formal planning methods are not useful for the project since it is not large enough to apply CPM or PERT. They have utilized their experience for planning the website. Both members of the planning team took part in scores of the projects during the course of last ten years or so. They believe the project will be completed within specified time plus 10% discount for unavoidable circumstances.

There were number of issues to address at this stage: determining the duration, sequence and dependencies of activities, allocation of resources and assignments of activities to various teams or individuals, determination of milestones and control mechanism.

Management of the project has been accomplished with the passage of time and with the progress of work.

Since the endeavor will be completed in three months, the duration of activities has been estimated based on the past experience; they are shown in table 2 below.

Table 2 Duration of Activities (in men-hours)

Activities	Code number	Duration
Index page	EG1	4
Banners	EG2	15
Slides	EG3	4
Marquees	EG4	4
Frames	EG5	12
Search (Query box)	EG6	2
Products	EG7	2
Services	EG8	2
Text box	EG9	292
Hyperlinks	EG10	74
Color	EG11	2

The total numbers of men-hours needed were spread over the life of the project since the project will be accommodated as an addition to existing workload i.e., ., as a part time endeavor.

However individual activities were distributed to all team members. Table 3 depicts the distribution of workload.

Table 3 Allocation of activities to team members

Members	Activities to work	Total workload
Jones	Banners, homepage, slides, and marquees	27
Yong	Text boxes	292
Shan	Hyperlinks and Frames	86

| **Fast** | Colors and search boxes | 4 |
| **Long** | Products and services | 4 |

In addition to that everyone must know the sequence of activities and dependencies that is helpful to visualize the project over its life cycle. Mr. Long did it for other members and he has drawn it in table 4.

Table 4 Sequence and dependencies of activities

Activity	Predecessor
EG.1	None
EG.2	**Eg1**
EG.3	**Eg2**
EG.4	**Eg3**
EG.5	**Eg1**
EG.6	**Eg5**
EG.7	**Eg6, Eg4**
EG.8	**Eg6, Eg4**
EG.9	**Eg8**
EG.10	**Eg9**
EG.11	**Eg10**

The table may be the basics of developing the network diagram to depict all the activities (Figure 1).

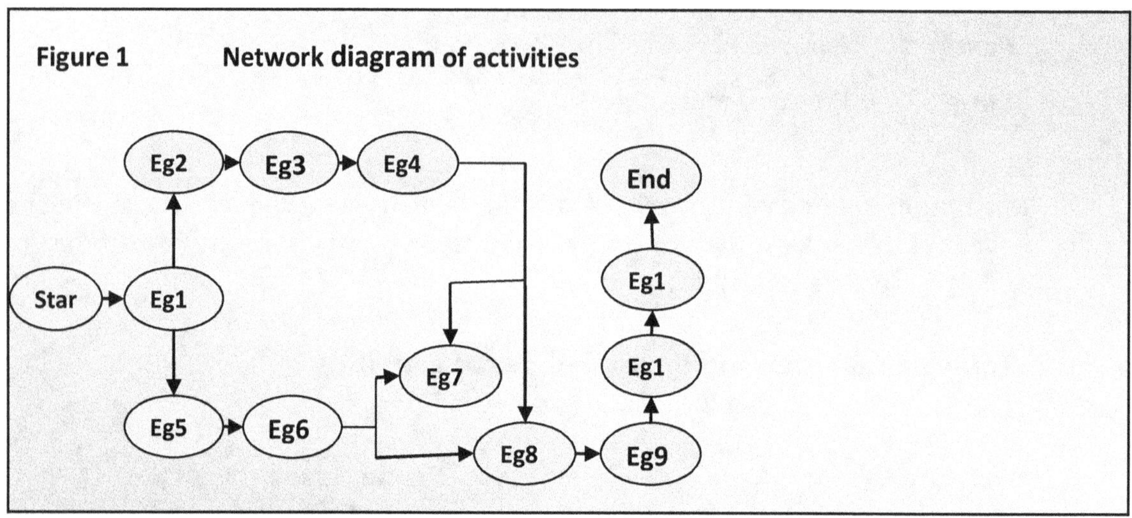

It is further elaborated with the addition of duration of activities which may be used for determination of critical path. Figure 2 depicts activities with duration in terms of men-hours required to complete various activities.

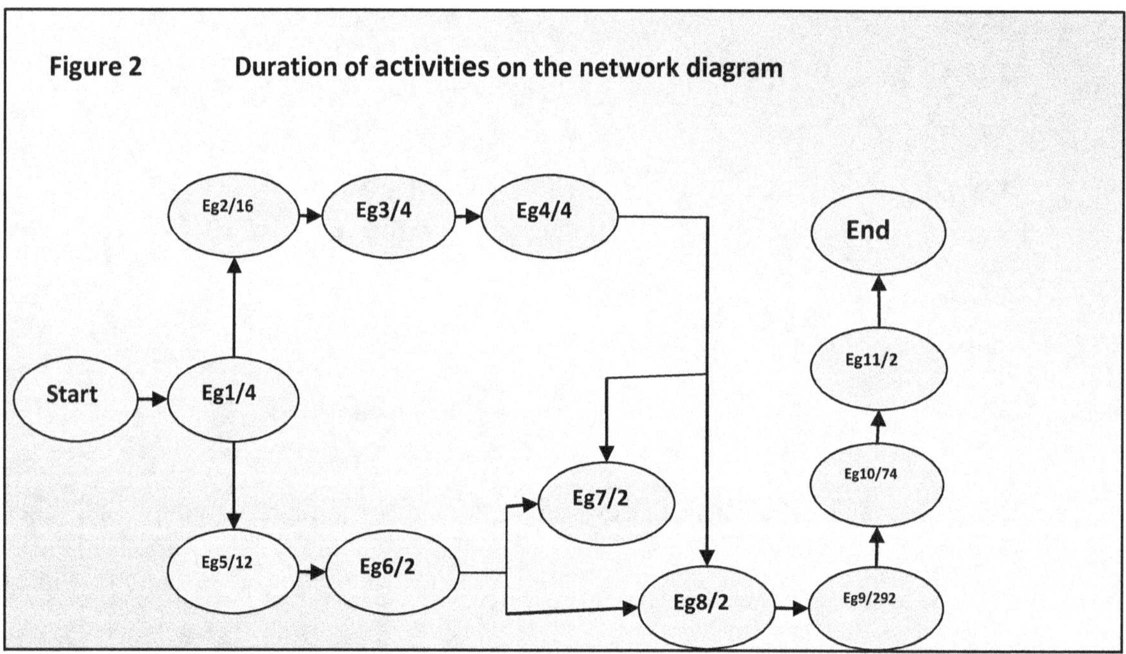

The critical path has been calculated in Table 5. The third alternative is the longest path and takes maximum time to complete.

Table 5 Calculation of critical path

Activities	Alternative 1	Alternative 2	Alternative 3
1	4	4	4
2	16	0	16
3	4	0	4
4	4	0	4
5	0	12	0
6	0	2	0
7	0	2	2
8	2	2	2
9	292	292	292
10	74	74	74
11	2	2	2
Total	398	390	400

Therefore, it is the critical path. The dependencies have been determined according to the nature of the project. For example, home page is designed so that other features can be created upon it. And the hyperlinks are developed when sub files (supporting files) are created and so on.

Since all the resources for the development of a website are shared; all the members work on more than one project at a time, and they use resources as and when they need them. For instance, printers are shared, however each member of the staff owns a PC, which is installed on his desk and dedicated to him. It suggests that no special arrangements are required for the project.

Some project does need new resources, but it is associated with the nature of the project. However, budget is set aside for each project for internal evaluation and control purpose.

The length of the project has been determined in man-hours; the calculation of cost is also ascertained accordingly. Each men-hour cost £500 to the company, the cost of each activity is shown in Table-6. Although there are variations in the reward of personnel involved yet a flat rate is applied for cost calculation for the sack of simplicity and convenience.

Reporting and Control Mechanism

It is widely believed that planning looks forward and control looks back i.e., . what has been done and how that is done. Control involves   determining timings of reports and deciding what reports are required to measure the progress of a project. The responsibilities are fixed for the

Table 6 Determination of Cost			
Activity	**Duration**	**Rate**	**Activity Cost**
EG.1	4	£500/men-hour	£ 2000
2	16	"	8000
3	4	"	2000
4	4	"	2000
5	12	"	6000
6	2	"	1000
7	2	"	1000
8	2	"	1000
9	292	"	146,000
10	74	"	37,000
11	2	"	1,000
Total			**207,000**

collection of data, analysis and communication of results to the relevant authorities. The project sponsor is usually the audience of such reports. The team members may prepare the reports or independent parties can be appointed for the purpose. The independent parties may be within the organization or external organization may be hired. Sometimes the clients are also involved in the progress monitoring team.

The progress is checked at regular intervals such as weekly, fortnightly, or monthly basis; milestones and or major activities are also possible in project management. Maturity gates are also applicable in some projects. Eagles use milestones as a principle-reporting event for the project as a whole; individual performance is measured for each team member. It is important because team members usually work on more than on project at a time. Therefore, their progress is required. For instance, the weekly performance report for Jones shows the projects on which he worked, and the time spent on each of it. (Table-7)

Table 7 Weekly progress report of Mr. Jones

Projects	Allocated time for the project	Work completed	Work in balance
EG	28 men-hours	4	24
EM	58	12	46
EF	122	2	120
EB	60	10	50
ES	12	12	0
Total	**280**	**40**	**240**

The progress of projects is also reported on weekly basics about the completion of various activities and or if a milestone has been reached. A weekly report has been prepared for the first week of the project under discussion. Table 8 shows the details.

Table 8 Progress report of activities.

Activities Completed	Time worked	Total project time	Balance
EG 1	4 hours		
EG 2	16		
EG3	4		
Total	28	414	386
Total %	**7%**		**93%**

The project planning and organizing were completed but the outcome yet to be seen. Several issues emerged when implementation was on the way to reality. The person in charge of hyperlinks left the company because he has been offered a better position in the neighboring firm. A new guy was employed to replace him; however, the employment process took four weeks i.e., advertise, screen, interview, select and induct. He was an experience person but unable to cope with the lost time. It caused to delay the entire project by one week and increased the cost by £20,000 which reduced the return on investment below industry level. The customer was compensated for the loss of time with a reduction in the total price of the project; it added another £10,000 to the total cost. In addition, Eagles were unable to start another project which was in pipeline at that time. It also created an implied cost that increased the fixed cost related to development of all projects which used to be distributed over all projects in the current fiscal year. It was the first project since the start of the company which derailed from the plan substantially. Management believed that it would have far reaching impacts on profitability, productivity, and image of the organization. Therefore, a team was set up to find the causes of delay in addition to the resignation of the person in charge of hyperlinks. The purpose was to redefine the project management strategy in the future based upon the findings of the current experience. The person in charge of the investigation must give the report within two weeks.

Case question

1. The project overrun triple constrains i.e., cost, time of delivery and quality. Do you agree? If not, why?

2. Does the resignation of the person in charge of the hyperlinks, the only reason of the project delay?

3. What were the other reasons of failure (if any) and how they could be avoided?

4. The company lost money, creditability, and many more assets. What were they? Could they be saved?

5. If you were the person in charge of the investigation team and your research revealed that in addition to the personnel issues, there were project management problems in the case. What amendments do you suggest being included in the future business or project management strategy?

4 THE HIJRAH EXPEDITION OF THE PROPHET (ﷺ)

Introduction

The Prophet (ﷺ) had initiated and completed many endeavours which can be classified as management of the project. His major project was the introduction of Islam to the world. He had also defined and completed many military and social projects. Hijrah was also a project. Iqbal and Ahmad had discussed it as an implementation of a planning model[2] and Iqbal Saani had worked it as a case study in planning.[3] According to PMI, it also fulfils the condition of a project; therefore, the chapter is reserved for it in this treatise.

Hijrah was the marvellous project after the introduction of Islam in the life of the Prophet (ﷺ). It turned the tides of the history, laid down the foundation for the first Islamic state on the earth. It became the capital of Islam for years to is a source of blessing for Muslims today.

The Hijrah was not a matter of changing geographical location, but it was for the pleasure of Allah (SWT). Consider the hadith,

It is narrated on the authority of Amirul Mu'minin, Abu Hafs 'Umar bin al-Khattab (رضي الله عنه) who said: I heard the Messenger of Allah (ﷺ) say: "Actions are (judged) by motives (niyyah), so each man will have what he intended. Thus, he whose migration (Hijrah) was to Allah and His Messenger, his migration is to Allah and His Messenger; but he whose migration was for some worldly thing he might gain, or for a wife he might marry, his migration is to that for which he migrated." [Bukhari & Muslim; Riyadus Saleheen, Abridged Edition, p. 5]

It was also the fact of the history that whosoever migrated from Makkah for the sake of Allah (SWT), he/she never returned.

A project is an initiative which has a beginning and an end which achieves an objective (s). It involves one or more individuals and requires some resources on the part of the manager or the boss. The Hijrah encompass all the elements. So, let us look at Hijrah as a project.

2 Iqbal, Javed and Muhammad Mushtaq Ahmad (2009) Planning in the Islamic Tradition: The Case of Hijrah Expedition, INSIGHT, 1(3), 37-68.

3 Saani, Javed Iqbal (2018) Managerial Thoughts of the Prophet (ﷺ), Intellectual Capital Enterprise Limited, London, available on amazon (Paperback edition).

What is a project?

For a layperson a project is "an individual or collaborative enterprise that is carefully planned to achieve a particular aim."[4] Project Management Institute (PMI) defines a project as "A project is temporary in that it has a defined beginning and end in time, and therefore defined scope and resources.

And a project is unique in that it is not a routine operation, but a specific set of operations designed to accomplish a singular goal."[5]

The Hijrah is a project because it has a beginning time and an ending time. It had a defined scope and resources. And it was not a routine matter; it happened only once in the life of the Prophet (ﷺ). It involved a specific set of operations and it had achieved a clearly defined objective.

Justification of Hijrah as a project

Let me explain the above elements or part of Hijrah which defined it as a project.

The beginning and ending time

If we look at the timing of it, it began a long time ago. Prophet (ﷺ) went to the people of Yathrib in Mina during Hajj; invited them towards Islam and asked them that he needs a place where he could do his job peacefully. Molana Yousaf Kandhelvi writes in this connection,

Hadhrat Aa'isha (رضي الله عنها) says, "Every year Rasulullaah (ﷺ) used to present his case to the various Arab tribes, asking them to grant him asylum with their people so that he could propagate Allaah's word and message. He promised them Jannah in return for their assistance. However, no Arab tribe accepted his offer until the time came when Allaah decided that His Deen should become dominant, that his Nabi (ﷺ) should receive assistance and that His promises should be fulfilled. It was then that Allaah pulled forward the tribe of the Ansaar. They accepted the offer of Rasulullaah (ﷺ) and Allaah thus created a place to which Rasulullaah (ﷺ) could migrate."[6]

4 https://www.google.com/search?q=what+is+a+p
roject&oq=What+is+a+project&aqs=chrome.0.0l6.1 3948j0j8&sourceid=chrome&ie=UTF-8

5 https://www.pmi.org/about/learn-aboutpmi/what-is-project-management

6 P. 374.

The Prophet (ﷺ) also sent his companions to Abyssinia for the purpose and he travelled to Taif for the same reason, but he could not receive positive result.

We understand that the Hijrah was the outcome of the treaty that took place between the Prophet (ﷺ) and the Muslims of Madinah. The Prophet (ﷺ) allowed his followers to emigrate to the new place. Most of them reached Yathrib. However, the Prophet (ﷺ) was waiting for the Devine signal. Soon after it he commenced the preparations and planned the journey with the consultation of Abu Bakr (رضي الله عنه). Meanwhile, the pagans conspired for his assassination. Mubarikpuri has recorded the starting time; he states, "The Prophet (ﷺ) had thus left his house on Safar 27th, the fourteenth year of Prophethood, i.e., ., 12/13 September 622 A.D."[7] The noble team arrived in Madinah after about ten days. It was Monday, 8th Rabi 'Al-Awwal, the 14th year of Prophethood; the September 23rd 622.[8] His first destination was Quba, the suburb of Madinah.

Scope and resources

Project scope is the "the extent of the area or subject matter that something deals with or to which it is relevant."[9] PMBOK guide defines it as "the work performed to deliver a product, service or result with specified features and functions."[10]

Implications of the first definition are that the subject matter of the Hijrah was to travel from Makkah to Madinah. The second definition indicates the feature of the service. The feature of the service was safety and convenience. The noble team completed their journey safely. Taking into consideration the level of technological and scientific development i.e., the conveyance available and the guide of the journey, both were of high quality. Each of the members of the team was using a camel for travel. The camel is considered as the ship of the desert than and even now. The other element was the modern "Navigation System", a reliable guide was hired for this purpose.

As for as the resources are concerned, Iqbal and Ahmad reported seven individuals were involved in the expedition. Two she-camels were used, and food supplies were taken for a few days.

Unique operations

The other aspect of the expedition was that it was a one-off endeavour (it was a temporary initiative). As the definition says it is not a routine operation it is a set of

---

7 P. 85, The English Translation.

8 P. 86, The English Translation.

9 https://en.oxforddictionaries.com/definition/sco pe

10 PMI (2017) PMBOK Guide, Pennsylvania: Project Management Institute.

operations to accomplish a goal/object. The noble team performed many operations. For instance, the Prophet (ﷺ) formed a team, hired a guide, ensure supply of food, travelled to a cave, stayed there for a couple of days, and finally took a long journey to reach Madinah. The purpose of Quraysh was to harm the Prophet (ﷺ) or the noble team, but they did not do it. On the contrary, the noble team achieved its objective. Thus, the Prophet (ﷺ) made the plan of the opponents fail and achieved his objective. It suggests that the endeavour was a set of operations.

Project life cycle

The Hijrah started on the first day of the Hijrah calendar and ended at eighth year of Hijrah. Therefore, it remained in operation for about eight years.

According to PMI "a project life cycle is the series of phases that a project passes through from its start to completion."[11] There are four generic phases of a project: starting, organising, and preparing, carrying out the work, and closing the project. Let us take them in turn with reference to the topic.

Since it was a small project compared to some of the contemporary projects such as the construction of a dam or an airport, therefore, our discussion would be short. In addition, the scope of the book does not allow me to inject a large amount of material to understand the phenomenon. It is a sample from the life of the Prophet (ﷺ) so that we can understand the subject. The purpose is to show the reality that the Prophet (ﷺ) had managed the project. And he did it successfully. The project under discussion is a non-military initiative. We know that he had to launch many military projects for self-defence. We know that Quraysh commenced first three major military encounters. Consequently, he had to defend armless people, women, children, and old people from the brutalities of his opponents.

Starting the Hijrah

The seeds of the Hijrah were planted when the people of Yathrib embraced Islam in the 11th year of the Prophethood. They technically pledged to the Prophet (ﷺ) to do anything for the sake of Islam. It concluded at the famous pact between Muslims of Madinah and the Prophet (ﷺ). Lings provides the details of the treaty, he states

After reciting from the Koran and pronouncing a summons to God and to Islam, the Prophet (ﷺ) said: "I make with you this pact on condition that the allegiance ye pledge me shall bind you to protect me even as ye *protect* your women and your children." Bara' rose and took his hand and said: "By Him who sent thee with the truth, we will protect

11 PMI (2017) PMBOK Guide, Pennsylvania: Project Management Institute.

thee as we protect them. So, accept the pledge of our allegiance, o Messenger of God, for we are men of war, possessed of arms that have been handed down from father to son." A man of Aws then broke in upon him and said: "o Messenger of God, there are ties between us and other men" - he meant the Jews - "and we are willing to sever them. But might it not be that if we do this, and if then God gives thee victory, thou wilt return to thy people and leave us?" The Prophet (ﷺ) smiled and said: "Nay, I am yours and ye are mine. Whom ye war against, him I war against. Whom ye make peace with him I make peace with."[12]

It paved the way for the Prophet (ﷺ) to allow his followers to leave Makkah and join their brethren in Madinah. The Prophet (ﷺ) permitted his companions to start the movement. It took most of them about two months to reach the new home. In project management terms it was the **first milestone**.

Many houses in Makkah become empty or the dweller could be counted on fingers by the birth of the second moon.

Nevertheless, the Prophet (ﷺ) was waiting for the Divine permission. People in Madinah were also waiting for him. The hours of patience ended; Quraysh made a killer plan and Allah (SWT)

(SWT) permitted the Prophet (ﷺ) to move ahead. Preparations were already made; Abu Bakr (رضي الله عنه) arranged transport and a guide was hired. Quraysh sieged the house of the Prophet (ﷺ) so that as soon as the Prophet (ﷺ) waked up for the morning prayers, the warriors would complete their mission. The Prophet (ﷺ) walked through their lines, but they were made blind for a while until they lost their prey. The Prophet (ﷺ) walked to Abu Bakr (رضي الله عنه), and they stepped out towards a cave.

Organising, and preparing

According to Kreitner (2009), Organising encompasses chain of command, the division of labour and assignment of responsibilities to individuals and teams.[13] Let us see the way of the Prophet (ﷺ) to organise the Hijrah expedition.

The dictionary meaning of the chain of command is that it is "a system in a military or civil organization by which instructions are passed from one person to another." And in business terms, it is "The order in which authority and power in an organization are wielded and delegated from top management to every employee at every level of the

12 P.111.

13 P. 239.

organization. Instructions flow downward along the chain of command and accountability flows upward."[14]

Iqbal and Ahmad (2009) state that there were seven persons involved in the expedition. The Prophet (ﷺ) was managing the project. Abu Bakr was functioning as deputy. Saani (2018) enumerates other members and their functions i.e., .

1.   Ali ibn-e-Talib (رضي الله عنه) (Representative of Rasulullaah (ﷺ) in Makkah)

2.   Abdullah bin Abu Bakr (رضي الله عنه) (Information officer)

3.   Aamir bin Fuhayra (رضي الله عنه) (The Shepherd)

4.   Ibnul Ayqadh (The guide)

Asma bint Abu Bakr (رضي الله عنها) (Food maker) [15]

 Formation of a team is the starting point of a project who normally prepare the organisation for the project. The Prophet (ﷺ) formed the initial team of himself and Abu Bakr (رضي الله عنه). Lings[270] at this occasion draw the picture of the way the Prophet (ﷺ) had formed the team after receiving Divine instruction for the journey. He puts it in the following words.

It was noon, an unusual time for visiting, but the Prophet (ﷺ) went straight to the house of Abu Bakr who knew at once, as soon as he saw him at that hour, that something important had happened. 'A'ishah and her elder sister Asma' were with their father when the Prophet (ﷺ) came in. "God hath allowed me to leave the city and to emigrate," he said. "Together with me?" said Abu Bakr. "Together with thee," said the Prophet (ﷺ). 'A'ishah was at that time in her seventh year. She used to say afterwards: "I knew not before that day that one could weep for joy until I saw Abu Bakr weep at those words." The team was expanded later to include other members. Four members travelled towards Madinah.[16] Similarly, four members were functional during the stay of the team in the cave: Aamir bin Fuhayra (رضي الله عنه) (the shepherd), Abdullah bin Abu Bakr (رضي الله عنه), the intelligence officer in addition to the Prophet (ﷺ) himself and Abu Bakr (رضي الله عنه). The Prophet (ﷺ) was coordinating the entire project. Since the migration was in sight, therefore, Abu Bakr (رضي الله عنه) who was a friend, and loyal

---

14 http://www.businessdictionary.com/definition/c hain-of-command.html

15 Saani, Prof Dr Javed Iqbal (2018) Planning Strategy of the Prophet (ﷺ), Intellectual Capital Enterprise Limited, London, available on amazon (Paperback edition) 270 p. 116.

16 Mubarikpuri, p. 233.

companion was waiting for the Hijrah. He wanted to leave Makkah, but the Prophet (ﷺ) asked him to wait. He also prepared two she-camels for the journey: one for him and the other for the Prophet (ﷺ). In the words of Lings "Abu Bakr (رضي الله عن ه) had asked the Prophet (ﷺ)'s permission to emigrate, but he had said: "Hasten not away, for it may be that God will give thee a companion." So, Abu Bakr (رضي الله عن ه) understood that he must wait for the Prophet (ﷺ), and he gave orders for two of his camels to be fed on gum acacia leaves in preparation for their journey to Yathrib."[17] The preparations were deliberate and well planned. It led the project towards the valley of success.

Carrying out the work

The phase is about the actual work done or implementation of what was planned?   The execution commenced with the journey of the Prophet (ﷺ). He appointed Ali (رضي الله عنه) as his representative to return the safe keeping of people i.e., the property they left with the Prophet (ﷺ) for safe keeping because people knew him trustworthy. He left his home and walked towards the residence of Abu Bakr (رضي الله عن ه). It was midnight. Both took an exit from a back-side window. Walked towards the Southern side, towards Yemen.

According to the plan they would stay in the cave for a couple of days. The purpose was to wait for a search to die out because Quraysh wanted to capture them. Molana Yusaf Kandhelvi writes,

They stayed three nights in the cave and every evening Hadhrat Aamir bin Fuhayra (رضي الله عنه) would bring the goats of Hadhrat Abu Bakr (رضي الله عنه) to them. At night, he would take them back and by the morning they would be grazing with the shepherds in the grazing lands. Hadhrat Amir (رضي الله عنه) used to return the goats in the evening with the other shepherds but would walk very slowly (so that he would be left behind) and then take the goats to Hadhrat Abu Bakr (رضي الله عنه) once the night became dark. Hadhrat Abdullaah (رضي الله عنه) the son of Hadhrat Abu Bakr (رضي الله عنه) used to spend the day in Makkah finding out the news and then inform

Rasulullaah (ﷺ) and Hadhrat Abu Bakr (رضي الله عنه) about this when he met them at night. He then left them late at night and was in Makkah by the dawn.[18]

It implies that there was an arrangement of food and information about the activities of Quraysh. Molana Yusaf continued the description of the story and states,

17 P. 114.

18 P. 341-42.

(After three nights) Rasulullah (ﷺ) and Hadhrat Abu Bakr (رضي الله عنه) left the cave and took a route along the coast. Hadhrat Abu Bakr (رضي الله عنه) travelled in front of Rasulullaah (ﷺ) but whenever he felt any danger from the rear, he travelled at the back. The entire journey passed in this manner. Hadhrat Abu Bakr (رضي الله عن ه) was a well-known man. Therefore, whenever someone met him, they asked who was with him. He would reply, **"He is a guide who is showing me the way."** By saying this, he meant that Rasulullaah (ﷺ) was guiding him in Deen, but the person thought that Rasulullaah (ﷺ) was someone showing him the road.[19]

The project was running amicably. But one of the opponents was following the noble team to earn the huge reward announce in Makkah for the capture of the noble team. Abu Bakr (رضي الله عن ه) tells us more details.

"Although people were searching for us, no one caught up with us besides Suraaqa bin Maalik bin Ju'shum, who did so on his horse. (Seeing him approach,) I said, "O Rasulullaah (ﷺ) here comes someone in search of us. He has caught up with us.' Rasulullaah (ﷺ) said, 'Do not grieve because Allaah is with us.' When Suraaqa drew close and was only the distance of one or two spear lengths away from us, I cried and said, 'o Rasulullaah (ﷺ) w! He has caught up with us!' Rasulullaah (ﷺ) asked, 'What makes you weep?' I replied, 'I swear by Allaah that it is not for my own safety that I weep but I am crying for your safety.' Rasulullaah (ﷺ) then made du'aa saying, 'o Allaah! Deal with him on our behalf as You please.' Suraaqa's horse suddenly sank into the ground up to its belly although the ground was hard. Suraaqa sprang off the horse and said, 'o Muhammad! I know that you have done this. Please pray to Allaah to save me from this predicament and I swear by Allaah that I shall throw every other tracker I meet off your trail. Take an arrow from my quiver here and when you pass by a certain place where you will see my camels and goats (show this arrow to the shepherds) and take whatever you need.' Rasulullah (ﷺ) said, 'I have no need for that.' Rasulullaah (ﷺ) then made du'aa to Allaah and Suraaqa was freed. He then returned to his people."[20]

It implies there was an obstacle on the way of the project, but the Prophet (ﷺ) overcome it with the help of Allah (SWT). Here the Prophet (ﷺ) had taken corrective action because the project was derailing from the plan. He put the project on the original track.

In project management terms it was *another milestone*. The Prophet (ﷺ) took his team and himself out of the jaws of opponents. The project could end here if the team were to be caught. But with the help of Allah (SWT) the Prophet (ﷺ) remained safe, steadfast, and successful to take the project to the next stage.

19 P.343.

20 P. 345.

The journey was continued as per plan. So, let us see the final phase of the project.

Completing the project

The project was partially completed when the noble team reached Madinah without a major obstruction.   One of the most important milestones of the project ended with the arrival of the Prophet (ﷺ) in Madinah. Lings beautifully draw the scene of Prophet (ﷺ)'s entry in Madinah.

Several days previously news from Mecca of the Prophet (ﷺ)'s disappear of Quba' were expecting him daily, for the time of his arrival was now overdue; so every morning, after the dawn prayer, some of the Bani 'Amr would go out to look for him, and with them went men of other clans who lived in that village, and also those of the emigrant Quraysh who were still there and had not yet moved to Medina. They would go out beyond the fields and palm groves onto the lava tract, and after they had gone some distance, they would stop and wait until the heat of the sun became fierce; then they would return to their homes. They had gone out that morning but had already returned by the time the four travellers had begun their descent of the rocky slope. Eyes were no longer staring expectantly in that direction; but the sun shone on the new white garments of the Prophet (ﷺ) and Abu Bakr which were set off more against the background of bluish-black volcanic stones, and a Jew who happened to be on the roof of his house caught sight of them. He knew at once who they must be, for the Jews of Quba' had asked and been told why so many of their neighbours had taken to going out in a body into the wilderness every morning without fail. So, he called out at the top of his voice: "Sons of Qaylah, he has come, he is come!" The call was immediately taken up, and men, women and children hurried from their houses and streamed out once more onto the strip of greenery which led to the stone track. But they had not far to go, for the travellers had by now reached the most outlying palm-grove. It was a noon of extraordinary joy on all sides, and the Prophet (ﷺ) addressed them, saying: "o people, give unto one another greetings of Peace; feed food unto the hungry; honour the ties of kinship; pray in the hours when men sleep. Even so, shall ye enter Paradise in Peace."[21]

The arrival of the noble team in Madinah was the **second milestone** of the project. Thus, the project completed its major objective with the joy of Muslims both to the migrants of Makkah and blessed souls of Madinah. The sacrifice of Makkan and open-hearted welcome of Muslims of Madinah made the new place a centre of guidance for the rest of the time.

21 P. 120.

Monitoring the project

There were many Muslims still in Makkah. The stipulations of the treaty of Hodhabia included that any person migrating from Makkah to Madinah shall be returned. The Prophet (ﷺ) had returned many companions accordingly. One of the stories of Abu Jandal was notable, Imam Bukhari narrates that "Then Suhail said, "We also stipulate that you should return to us whoever comes to you from us, even if he embraced your religion." The Muslims said, "Glorified be Allah! How will such a person be returned to the pagans after he has become a Muslim? While they were in this state Abu- Jandal bin Suhail bin `Amr came from the valley of Mecca staggering with his fetters and fell amongst the Muslims. Suhail said, "O Muhammad! This is the very first term with which we make peace with you, i.e., ., you shall return Abu Jandal to me." The Prophet (ﷺ) said, "The peace treaty has not been written yet." Suhail said, "I will never allow you to keep him." The Prophet (ﷺ) said, "Yes, do." He said, "I won't do.: Mikraz said, "We allow you (to keep him)."[22] Similarly Abu Baseer (رضي الله عن ه) was also returned.[23] In addition, many people were in Abyssinia at the time of the grand Hijrah; they joined the Prophet (ﷺ) in Madinah later direct from Abyssinia.

Closing the Hijrah chapter

A project is closed when objectives are achieved, an artefact is manufactured, or a construction project is completed and handed over to the owners. New product development projects bring a brand-new artefact to the existing portfolio or product lines of the organisation concerned.

Since the order of Muslim was established at the time of conquering of Makkah which necessitated to close the chapter of Hijrah. We understand that Hijrah was compulsory when Muslims were living in the non-Muslim controlled territory. It was, therefore, difficult for them to practice Islam properly. At that time, Muslims were persecuted in Makkah, so, the Hijrah was announced/commenced.

The Prophet (ﷺ) had closed the project at the occasion of the conquest of Makkah. "Narrated Ibn `Abbas: Allah's Messenger (ﷺ) said, "There is no Hijra (i.e., migration) (from Mecca to Medina) after the Conquest (of Mecca), but Jihad and good intention remain; and if you are called (by the Muslim ruler) for fighting, go forth immediately."[24]

22 Sahih al-Bukhari, Vol. 3, Book 50, Hadith 891.

23 Kandhelvi, Muhammad Zakarya, Faial-e-Amaal, p. 24-25.

24 Sahih al-Bukhari, Vol. 4, Book 52, Hadith 42.

In project management language it was the **third milestone** of the project. We learned a couple of points about the topic. We assumed at the beginning that Hijrah was a project. It fulfils all the conditions of being a project in the contemporary terms. Secondly, the Prophet (ﷺ) had managed it with an immense success. He initiated the project, managed it, and closed it. The unique aspect of the project was the Devine assistance. When the opponents were planning for his assassination, the angel informed him. Consequently, he planned the project. Thus, defeated the enemy. Their plans were failed. His objective was to leave Makkah peacefully and reach Madinah. And he did it.

Case questions

1. Why hijrah was a project as perceived in modern terms?
2. Does starting and ending dates are the only parameter to be a project?
3. How different is hijrah project from others case studies?
4. Critically examine hijrah as a project.

REFERENCES

Ahmad, Ammar et al, 2007. A review of techniques for risk management in projects, Benchmarking: An International Journal, Vol. 14, No. 1, pp. 22-36.

Alshawi, Mustafa and Bingunath Ingirige 2003. Web-enabled project management: an emerging paradigm in construction, *Automation in Construction*, Vol. 12, pp. 349-364.

Ambler, Scott W. 2008. IT Project Success Rates Survey Results: August 2007, http://www.drdobbs.com.

Andersen, E S, Kristoffer V Grude and Tor Haug 1995. Goal Directed Project Management, Kogan Page, London.

Andersen Erling S. and Anne Live Vaagaasar 2009 Project Management Improvement Efforts—Creating Project Management Value by Uniqueness or Mainstream Thinking? *Project Management Journal*, Vol. 40, No. 1, pp. 19–27.

Azzopardi, Sandro. The Evolution of Project Management, Available at: http://www.buzzle.com/articles/evolution-project, Accessed 21 June 2010.

Baldry, D. 1998. The evaluation of risk management in public sector capital projects, International Journal of Project Management Vol. 16, No. 1, pp. 35-41.

Baker, M.J. 2000. Writing a Research Proposal, *The Marketing Review,* l (1), pp. 61-75.

Boyatzis, R. E. & Kolb, D. A., 1995. *From learning styles to learning skills*: the executive skills profile, Journal of Managerial Psychology, Vol. 10, no. 5, pp.3-17

Cadman, K. 2002. English for Academic Possibilities: the research proposal as contested site in postgraduate genre pedagogy, *Journal of English for Academic Purposes*, 1(2), pp. 85 –104.

Canalys, 2010. Android smart phone shipments grow 886% year-on-year in Q2 2010, Available at: http://www.canalys.com/pr/2010/r2010081.html , Accessed 10 November 2010.

Conforto, E C and D C Amaral, 2010 Evaluating an agile method for planning and controlling innovative projects, Project Management Journal, Vol. 41, No. 2, pp. 73–80

Corlien, M. V. et al, 2003. Proposal Development and Fieldwork, Designing and conducting health systems research projects: volume 1, The International Development Research Centre (IDRC), Canada.

Cooke-Davies et al, Terence J. 2009, Project Management Systems: Moving Project Management from an Operational to a Strategic Discipline, *Project Management Journal*, Vol. 40, No. 1, 110–123.

Crawford, Lynn H and Lynn H Government and Governance: The Value of Project Management in the Public Sector, *Project Management Journal*, Vol. 40, No. 1, 73–87.

Evaristo, R. and P C van Fenema 1999. A typology of project management: emergence and evolution of new forms, *International Journal of Project Management* Vol. 17, No. 5, 275 – 28.

Ferns, D C 1991. Developments in programme management International Journal of Project Management, Vol. 9, No. 3, 148-156.

Franke, A. 1987. Risk analysis in project management, Project Management, Vol. 5. No. 1, pp. 29-34.

Ghauri, P. et al 1995. Research methods in business studies, London: Prentice Hall.

Glass, N. 1995. *Management Masterclass*, London: Nicholas Brealey Publishing.

Greg, H. 2008 Absolute Beginner's Guide to Project Management, Rough Cuts, 2nd Edition, QUE Publishing, Available at: www.Quepublishing.com, Accessed 10 June 2010.

Greg, H. 2005 Essential elements for managing any successful project, QUE Publishing, Available at: www.Quepublishing.com, Accessed 10 June 2010.

Hameri, Ari-Pekka 1997. Project management in a long-term and global one-of-a-kind project, *International Journal of Project Management* Vol. 15, No. 3, pp. 151-157.

Hartman, F and Greg Skulmoski 1999. Quest for Team competence,

International Journal of Project Management, Vol. 5, No. 1, pp. 10 – 15.

House, R S 1988. *The clean Side of Project Management,* Addison-Wesley, USA.

Haughty, Duncan 2010. A Brief History of Project Management, available at: http://www.projectsmart.co.uk/brief-history-of-project, Accessed 17 June 2010.

Iqbal J 2007. "Learning from a Doctoral Research Project: Structure and Content of a Research Proposal" *The Electronic Journal of Business Research Methods* Volume 5, Issue 1, 1 - 20, available online at www.ejbrm.com.

Jaafari, Ali 2001. Management of risks, uncertainties, and opportunities on projects: time for a fundamental shift, International Journal of Project Management Vol. 19, No. 2, pp. 89–101.

Johns, Thomas G 1995. Managing the behavior of people working in teams Applying the project-management method, International Journal of Project Management Vol. 13, No. 1, 33-38.

Juran, J M, 1989. Juran on *Leadership for Quality: An Executive Handbook*

Free Press, New York, NY.

Kotler, P. 2002. *Marketing Management*, London: Pearson Education.

Kuklan, H 1993. Effective Project Management: an expanded network approach, *Journal of Systems Management*, Vol. 44, No. 3,12-17.

Kumar, P.P. 2005. Effective use of Gantt chart for managing large scale projects, *Cost Engineering*, Vol. 47, No. 7, 14-21.

LaBrosse, M. 2008. 10 Ways to inspire your Team, Available at: www.project Smart.co.uk, Accessed 11 October 2010.

Mariosalexandrou, 2010, Project Manager Job Description, accessed 20 August, 2010, Available at http://www.mariosalexandrou.com/free-job-descriptions/project-manager.asp

Merchant, K. A. (1985) control in business organizations, Marshfield, MA: Pitman

Meredith, J. and S J Mantel 2010. *Project Management: A Managerial Approach, Singapore,* John Wiley & Sons.

Maylor, H. 2001. Beyond the Gantt chart Project management moving on. *European Management, Journal,* Vol. 19, No.1, 92–100.

Murphy, A and Ann Ledwith, 2007. Project management tools and techniques in high-technology SMEs, *Management Research News*, Vol. 30, No. 2,.153 – 166.

Nicholas, J M 2001. Project Management for Business and technology, principles and practices, New Dehli: Prentice-Hall of India Pvt. Ltd.

Nikander, I.O. and Eero Eloranta 2001. Project management by early warnings, *International Journal of Project Management* Vol. 19, No. 7, 385-399.

Omar, A. 2009. Uncertainty in Project Scheduling— Its Use in PERT/CPM Conventional Techniques, *Cost Engineering*, Vol. 51, No. 7, 30-34.

Perry, J G. 1986. Risk management - an approach for project managers, International Journal of Project Management, Vol. 4 No 4, pp. 211-221.

Project management institute (2000), A Guide to the Project Management Body of Knowledge (PMBOK Guide).

PROJECT MANAGEMENT INSTITUTE 2004. *A guide to the Project Management Body of Knowledge, 3rd ed.* Newton Square, PA: Project Management Institute.

PROJECT MANAGEMENT INSTITUTE 2010. Project institution documents, available at: www.mindtool.com, Accessed 21 June 2010.

Reiss, G. 1995. *Project Management Demystified*, Taylor & Francis.

Rozenez, S. et al 2004. MPCS: Multidimensional Project Control Systems, *International Journal of Project Management*, Vol. 22, No. 2, 109 – 118.

Saladis, Frank P. 2003. Taming the Wild Project -- Control Techniques for Project Success, available at: http://www.allpm.com/modules.php?op=modload&name=News&file=article&sid=653, Accessed 10 June 2010.

Smith, M. 2007. *Fundamentals of Management*, London: The McGraw Hill Companies.

Soderlund, J. 2004. Building Theories of Project management: past research, questions for the future, *International Journal of Project Management*, Vol. 22, No. 2, 183 – 191.

Thomas, J., & Mullaly, M.2007. Understanding the value of project management: First steps on an inter- national investigation in search of value, *Project Management Journal, 38*(3), 74–89.

Thomas, J L and Mark Mullaly (2009) Explorations of Value: Perspectives of the Value of Project Management, Project Management Journal, Vol. 40, No. 1, 2–3.

UK Association of Project Management (APM), *Body of Knowledge* (BoK) Revised January 1995 (version 2), Available at: *www.apm.org.**uk**,* Accessed 21 June 2010.

Vordaweb, accessed 20 August 2010, Available at: www.vordweb.co.uk.

Ward, Stephen C and Chris B Chapman, 1995. Risk-management perspective on the project lifecycle, International Journal of Project Management Vol. 13, No. 3, pp. 145-149.

White, D and J. Fortune 2002. Current Practices in Projects management – en empirical study, *International Journal of Project Management*, Vol. 20, No. 5, 1 – 11.

Wilson, J M 2003. Gantt charts: a centenary appreciation, European Journal of Operational research, Vol. 149, No. 2, 430-437.

Zhai Li et al, (2009) Understanding the Value of Project Management from a Stakeholder's Perspective: Case Study of Mega-Project Management, Project Management Journal, Vol. 40, No. 1, 99–109.

Zwikael, O, Kazuo Shimizu, and Shlomo Globerson 2005. Cultural differences in project management capabilities: A field study, International *Journal of Project Management*, Vol. 23, No. 6, 454 – 462.

INDEX

OTHER BOOKS BY THE AUTHOR (S)

Extension of Islamic Management Style

1. Prof Dr. Javed Iqbal Saani (2022) **Managing Resistance to Change: The Approach of the Prophet (ﷺ),** Intellectual Capital Enterprise Limited, London, available on Amazon (Paperback edition)
2. Prof Dr. Javed Iqbal Saani (2022) **Islamic Perspective of Entrepreneurship**, Intellectual Capital Enterprise Limited, London, available on Amazon (Paperback edition)
3. Prof Dr. Javed Iqbal Saani (2021) **Learning of Managerial Ideas from Quran**, Intellectual Capital Enterprise Limited, London, available on Amazon (Paperback edition)
4. Prof Dr. Javed Iqbal Saani (2021) **Islamic Guidelines for Administrators**, Intellectual Capital Enterprise Limited, London, available on Amazon (Paperback edition)
5. Prof Dr. Javed Iqbal Saani (2020) **Principles of Islamic Management**, Intellectual Capital Enterprise Limited, London, available on Amazon (Paperback edition)

Discovery of Islamic Management Theory

6. Prof Dr. Javed Iqbal Saani (2020) **Introduction to Islamic Theory of Management**, Intellectual Capital Enterprise Limited, London, available on Amazon (Paperback edition)
7. Prof Dr. Javed Iqbal Saani (2021) **How I have Discovered Islamic Management Theory?** Intellectual Capital Enterprise Limited, London, available on Amazon (Paperback edition)

Investigations of related topics

8. Prof Dr. Javed Iqbal Saani (2021) **The Concept of Reward in Islamic Management Theory**, Intellectual Capital Enterprise Limited, London, available on Amazon (Paperback edition)

9. Prof Dr. Javed Iqbal Saani (2021) **The Value of Work in Islamic Management Theory**, Intellectual Capital Enterprise Limited, London, available on Amazon (Paperback edition)

10. Prof Dr. Javed Iqbal Saani (2020) **Decisions Making Approach of the Prophet [PBUH]**, Intellectual Capital Enterprise Limited, London, available on Amazon (Paperback edition)

11. Prof Dr. Javed Iqbal Saani (2020) **Problem Solving Approach of the Prophet [PBUH]**, Intellectual Capital Enterprise Limited, London, available on Amazon (Paperback edition)

12. Prof Dr. Javed Iqbal Saani (2020) **Prophet (ﷺ) Muhammad's [PBUH] Selection of Team Leaders**, Intellectual Capital Enterprise Limited, London, available on Amazon (Paperback edition)

13. Prof Dr. Javed Iqbal Saani (2020) **Key Managerial Decisions of the Prophet (ﷺ) [PBUH]**, Intellectual Capital Enterprise Limited, London, available on Amazon (Paperback edition)

14. Prof Dr. Javed Iqbal Saani (2020) **Prophet (ﷺ) Muhammad [PBUH] & Evolution of Management Theory**, Intellectual Capital Enterprise Limited, London, available on Amazon (Paperback edition)

Finding of Managerial Implications of Major Expeditions & Ideas

15. Prof Dr. Javed Iqbal Saani (2020) **Managerial Implications of Five Pillars of Islam**, Intellectual Capital Enterprise Limited, London, available on Amazon (Paperback edition)

16. Prof Dr. Javed Iqbal Saani (2020) **Managerial Implications of the Conquest of Khyber**, Intellectual Capital Enterprise Limited, London, available on Amazon (Paperback edition)

17. Prof Dr. Javed Iqbal Saani (2019) **Managerial Implications of the Major Expeditions of the Prophet (ﷺ) [PBUH]**, Intellectual Capital Enterprise Limited, London, available on Amazon (Paperback edition)

18. Prof Dr. Javed Iqbal Saani (2019) **Managerial Implications of the Major Military Expeditions of the Prophet (ﷺ) [PBUH]**, Intellectual Capital Enterprise Limited, London, available on Amazon (Paperback edition)

19. Prof Dr. Javed Iqbal Saani (2019) **Managerial Implications of the Major Non-Military Expeditions of the Prophet (ﷺ) [PBUH]**, Intellectual Capital Enterprise Limited, London, available on Amazon (Paperback edition)

20. Prof Dr. Javed Iqbal Saani (2019) **Managerial Implications of the Treaty of Hodhabia**, Intellectual Capital Enterprise Limited, London, available on Amazon (Paperback edition)

21. Prof Dr. Javed Iqbal Saani (2019) **Managerial Implications of the Battle of Trench**, Intellectual Capital Enterprise Limited, London, available on Amazon (Paperback edition)

22. Prof Dr. Javed Iqbal Saani (2019) **Managerial Implications of the Conquest of Makkah**, Intellectual Capital Enterprise Limited, London, available on Amazon (Paperback edition)

23. Prof Dr. Javed Iqbal Saani (2019) **Managerial Implications of the Battle of Hunain**, Intellectual Capital Enterprise Limited, London, available on Amazon (Paperback edition)

24. Prof Dr. Javed Iqbal Saani (2019) **Managerial Implications of the Battle of Uhadh Campaign**, Intellectual Capital Enterprise Limited, London, available on Amazon (Paperback edition)

25. Prof Dr. Javed Iqbal Saani (2019) **Managerial Implications of the Tabuk Campaign**, Intellectual Capital Enterprise Limited, London, available on Amazon (Paperback edition)

26. Prof Dr. Javed Iqbal Saani (2018) **Managerial Implications of the Hijrah Expedition**, Intellectual Capital Enterprise Limited, London, available on Amazon (Paperback edition)

27. Prof Dr. Javed Iqbal Saani (2018) **Managerial Implications of the Battle of BADR**, Intellectual Capital Enterprise Limited, London, available on Amazon (Paperback edition)

Consolidations of significant themes

28. Prof Dr. Javed Iqbal Saani (2021) **Project Management: An Islamic Perspective**, Intellectual Capital Enterprise Limited, London, available on Amazon (Paperback edition)

29. Prof Dr. Javed Iqbal Saani (2018) **Management Practices of Prophet Muhammad (ﷺ)**, Intellectual Capital Enterprise Limited, London, available on Amazon (Paperback edition)

30. Prof Dr. Javed Iqbal Saani (2020) **Transformation Strategy of the Prophet (ﷺ) [PBUH]**, Intellectual Capital Enterprise Limited, London, available on Amazon (Paperback edition)

31. Prof Dr. Javed Iqbal Saani (2019) **Financial Management Strategy of the Prophet (ﷺ) (PBUH)**, Intellectual Capital Enterprise Limited, London, available on Amazon (Paperback edition)

32. Prof Dr. Javed Iqbal Saani (2019) **Information Management Strategy of the Prophet (ﷺ) (PBUH)**, Intellectual Capital Enterprise Limited, London, available on Amazon (Paperback edition)

33. Prof Dr. Javed Iqbal Saani (2019) **Motivation Strategy of the Prophet (ﷺ) (PBUH)**, Intellectual Capital Enterprise Limited, London, available on Amazon (Paperback edition)

34. Prof Dr. Javed Iqbal Saani (2019) **Strategic Management: The Approach of the Prophet (ﷺ) (PBUH)**, Intellectual Capital Enterprise Limited, London, available on Amazon (Paperback edition)

Identification of Managerial functions

35. Prof Dr. Javed Iqbal Saani (2018) **Managerial Thoughts of the Prophet (ﷺ)**, Intellectual Capital Enterprise Limited, London, available on Amazon (Paperback edition)

36. Prof Dr. Javed Iqbal Saani (2018) **Controlling Strategy of the Prophet (ﷺ)**, Intellectual Capital Enterprise Limited, London, available on Amazon (Paperback edition)

37. Prof Dr. Javed Iqbal Saani (2018) **Leading Strategy of the Prophet (ﷺ)**, Intellectual Capital Enterprise Limited, London, available on Amazon (Paperback edition)

38. Prof Dr. Javed Iqbal Saani (2018) **Organising Strategy of the Prophet (ﷺ)**, Intellectual Capital Enterprise Limited, London, available on Amazon (Paperback edition)

39. Prof Dr. Javed Iqbal Saani (2018) **Planning Strategy of the Prophet (ﷺ)**, Intellectual Capital Enterprise Limited, London, available on Amazon (Paperback edition)

40. Prof Dr. Javed Iqbal Saani (2017) **Prophet Muhammad (ﷺ) as a planning expert**, available on Amazon (Paperback edition)

Specific topics

41. Prof Dr. Javed Iqbal Saani (2017) **Sales and Marketing: Selected Ahadith**, available on amazon.co.uk. (Paperback edition)

42. Prof Dr. Javed Iqbal Saani (2016) **Responsibilities of Managers: Selected Ahadith**, available on amazon.co.uk. (Paperback edition)

Management Sciences

1. Prof Dr. Javed Iqbal Saani (2019) Management Information Systems, Intellectual Capital Enterprise Limited, London, available on Amazon (Paperback edition)

2. Prof Dr. Javed Iqbal Saani (2018) Managing Your Projects, Intellectual Capital Enterprise Limited, London, available on amazon.co.uk. (Paperback edition)

3. Prof Dr. Javed Iqbal Saani (2017) Business Case Studies, Intellectual Capital Enterprise Limited, London, available on Amazon (Paperback edition)

4. Prof Dr. Prof Dr. Javed Iqbal Saani (2016) Research Proposals: Contents & Exemplars, available on amazon.co.uk. (Paperback edition)

5. Prof Dr Javed Iqbal Saani (2011) Digital Divide in South Asia, ISBN: 9789699578120.

6. Prof Dr. Javed Iqbal Saani and Muhammad Rafi Khattak (2011) Managing Risk in Projects, ISBN: 9789699578090.

7. Prof Dr. Javed Iqbal Saani and Muhammad Nadeem Khan (2011, 2018) Understanding Project Management, ISBN: 978969957845, available on Amazon (Paperback edition)

8. Prof Dr. Javed Iqbal Saani (2010) Managing strategic change: a real-world case study, ISBN: 978-3838330952, available on amazon.co.uk. (Paperback edition)

General Interest

1. Prof Dr. Javed Iqbal Saani (2021) **Key Topics in Islam**, Intellectual Capital Enterprise Limited, London, available on Amazon (Paperback & Kindle edition)

2. Prof Dr. Javed Iqbal Saani (2021) **Significance of Mosques in Islam**, Intellectual Capital Enterprise Limited, London, available on Amazon (Paperback edition)

3. Prof Dr. Javed Iqbal Saani (2021) **Rewards of Virtuous Deeds**, Intellectual Capital Enterprise Limited, London, available on Amazon (Paperback edition)

4. Prof Dr. Javed Iqbal Saani (2020) **Islamic Perspective of Knowledge**, Intellectual Capital Enterprise Limited, London, available on Amazon (Paperback edition)

5. Prof Dr. Javed Iqbal Saani (2019) The **Intercession of the Prophet (ﷺ)** (PBUH), Intellectual Capital Enterprise Limited, London, available on Amazon (Paperback edition)

6. Prof Dr. Javed Iqbal Saani (2019) **Who are Wrongdoers [Zalimoon]?** Intellectual Capital Enterprise Limited, London, available on Amazon (Paperback edition)

7. Prof Dr. Javed Iqbal Saani (2019) **Characteristics of Successful People**, Intellectual Capital Enterprise Limited, London, available on Amazon (Paperback edition)

8. Prof Dr. Javed Iqbal Saani (2019) **Key Campaigns of the Prophet [PBUH]**, Intellectual Capital Enterprise Limited, London, available on Amazon (Paperback edition)

9. Prof Dr. Javed Iqbal Saani (2019) **The Importance of Islamic Greeting**, Intellectual Capital Enterprise Limited, London, available on Amazon (Paperback edition)

10. Prof Dr. Javed Iqbal Saani (2019) **Who are Mujrimoon: Criminals, Polytheists & Sinners?** Intellectual Capital Enterprise Limited, London, available on Amazon (Paperback edition)

11. Prof Dr. Javed Iqbal Saani (2019) **GLAD TIDINGS of Allah (SWT) and His Apostle (PBUH) TO NOBLE PEOPLE**, Intellectual Capital Enterprise Limited, London, available on Amazon (Paperback edition)

12. Prof Dr. Javed Iqbal Saani (2019) **Qualities of Righteous People**, Intellectual Capital Enterprise Limited, London, available on Amazon (Paperback edition)

13. Prof Dr. Javed Iqbal Saani (2019) **Greatness of Allah (SWT) in the Words of Allah (SWT)**, Intellectual Capital Enterprise Limited, London, available on Amazon (Paperback edition)

14. Prof Dr. Javed Iqbal Saani (2019) **Tablighi Mazaakry: The Programme & Contents of the Work of Dawah**, Intellectual Capital Enterprise Limited, London, available on Amazon (Paperback edition)

15. Prof Dr. Javed Iqbal Saani (2018) **Qualities of Momins: The Quranic Perspective**, Intellectual Capital Enterprise Limited, London, available on Amazon (Paperback edition)

16. Prof Dr. Javed Iqbal Saani (2018) **Hajj Experience: Combining Dawah and Manasiks**, Intellectual Capital Enterprise Limited, London, available on Amazon (Paperback edition)

17. Prof Dr. Javed Iqbal Saani (2018) **Sukhn-e-Saani** (The book of poetry), Intellectual Capital Enterprise Limited, London, available on Amazon (Paperback edition)

18. Prof Dr. Javed Iqbal Saani (2017) **Virtues of Sickness: Selected Ahadith**, available on Amazon (Paperback edition)

19. Prof Dr. Javed Iqbal Saani (2017) **Muhammad (PBUH): His Trials & Tribulations**, available on Amazon (Paperback edition)

20. Prof Dr. Javed Iqbal Saani (2016) **Experience: The Journey of My Life**, available on amazon.co.uk. (Paperback edition)

NOTES